B

Garden Plants

for

North

Carolina

Pam Beck
Laura Peters

LONE
PINE

Lone Pine Publishing International

The Distributor: Lone Pine Publishing
1808 B Street NW, Suite 140
Auburn, WA, USA 98001
Website: www.lonepinepublishing.com

Library and Archives Canada Cataloguing in Publication

Beck Pam, 1953–
    Best garden plants for North Carolina / Pam Beck, Laura Peters.

Includes index.

ISBN–13: 978–976–8200–10–5
ISBN–10: 976–8200–10–3

    1. Plants, Ornamental—North Carolina. 2. Gardening—North Carolina.
I. Peters, Laura, 1968– II. Title.

SB453.2.N8B42 2006   635.9'09756   C2005–906489–7

Scanning & Electronic Film: Elite Lithographers Co.

Front cover photographs by Tim Matheson and Tamara Eder except where noted. *Clockwise from top right:* New Dawn rose, prunus, iris, Carolina silverbell, amaryllis (*Laura Peters*), daylily (*Allison Penko*), lily (*Laura Peters*), tickseed, lily (*Erika Flatt*).

Photography: All photos by Tim Matheson, Tamara Eder and Laura Peters except:
Pam Beck 91a&b, 119a&b; Joan de Grey 34a; Don Doucette 97b, 105b; Derek Fell 27a, 78a, 88a, 107a, 135a, 144a, 155a; Erika Flatt 134a, 159b; Anne Gordon 45b, 136b; Saxon Holt 27b, 58a, 78b, 112a&b, 135b, 136a, 144b; Duncan Kelbaugh 46a; Liz Klose 164a; Debra Knapke 122a; Colin Laroque 60b; Dawn Loewen 68b, 165a; Janet Loughrey 106, 107b; Marilynn McAra 130b; Kim O'Leary 18a&b, 45a, 56a, 61a, 86a, 139b; Allison Penko 10a, 102a, 104b, 117a, 123a, 126a&b, 129a, 152a, 153b, 157a&b, 164b; Photos.com 130a; Reiner Richter 110; Robert Ritchie 29a&b, 31b, 55a, 75 a&b, 94a, 108a, 139a; Peter Thompstone 15a, 47a, 170b; Mark Turner 53a, 70a&b, 148b, 155b; Don Williamson 128a&b; Tim Wood 54.

This book is not intended as a 'how-to' guide for eating garden plants. No plant or plant extract should be consumed unless you are certain of its identity and toxicity and of your potential for allergic reactions.

PC: P13

Table of Contents

Introduction 4

Annuals 11

Perennials 27

Trees & Shrubs 53

Roses 107

Vines 115

Bulbs, Corms & Tubers 125

Herbs 137

Ferns, Grasses & Groundcovers 147

Glossary 171
Index 172
Author Biographies and Acknowledgments . . 176

Introduction

Starting a garden can seem like a daunting task. Which plants should you choose? Where should you put them in the garden? This book is intended to give beginning gardeners the information they need to start planning and planting gardens of their own. It describes a wide variety of plants and provides basic planting information such as where and how to plant.

North Carolina exhibits a wide diversity of ecological regions, and each presents its own unique challenges. Each region has a temperature range that indicates relative hardiness. Consider this: 15° F is very different with snow cover or without; in soggy soil or in dry; following a hot summer or a long, cold, wet one. These factors will have more influence on the survival of plants than will temperature. Recognizing the type of climate in which you garden will help you determine hardiness. Your local garden center should be able to provide you with local hardiness zones and frost date information.

Hardiness zones and frost dates are two terms often used when discussing climate. Hardiness zones consider the temperatures and conditions in winter. Plants are rated based on the zones in which they grow successfully. The last-frost date in spring combined with the first-frost date in fall allows us to predict the length of the growing season.

Getting Started

When planning your garden, start with a quick analysis of the garden as it is now. Plants have different requirements, and it is best to put the right plant in the right place rather than to change your garden to suit the plants you want.

Knowing which parts of your garden receive the most and least amounts of sunlight will help you choose the proper plants and decide where to plant them. Light is classified into four basic groups: full sun (direct, unobstructed light all or most of the day); partial shade (direct sun for about half the day and shade for the rest); light shade (shade all or most of the day with some sun filtering through to ground level); and full shade (no direct sunlight). Most plants prefer a specific amount of light, but many can adapt to a range of light levels.

Plants use the soil to hold themselves upright but also rely on the many resources it holds: air, water, nutrients, organic matter and a host of microbes. The particle size of the soil influences the amount of air, water and nutrients it can hold. Sand, with the largest particles, has a lot of air space and allows water and nutrients to drain quickly. Clay, with the smallest particles, is high in nutrients but has very little air space. Water is therefore slow to penetrate clay and slow to drain from it.

Soil acidity or alkalinity (measured on the pH scale) influences the nutrients available to plants. A pH of 7 is neutral; a lower pH is more acidic. Most plants prefer a soil with a pH of 5.5–7.5. Soil-testing kits are available at most garden centers, and soil samples can be sent to testing facilities for a more thorough analysis.

Compost is one of the best and most important amendments you can add to any type of soil. Compost improves soil by adding organic matter and nutrients, introducing soil microbes, increasing water retention and improving drainage. Compost can be purchased or you can make it in your own backyard.

Microclimates are small areas that are generally warmer or colder than the surrounding area. Buildings, fences, trees and other large structures can provide extra shelter in winter but may trap heat in summer, thus creating a warmer microclimate. The bottoms of hills are usually colder than the tops but may not be as windy. Take advantage of these

Hardiness Zones Map

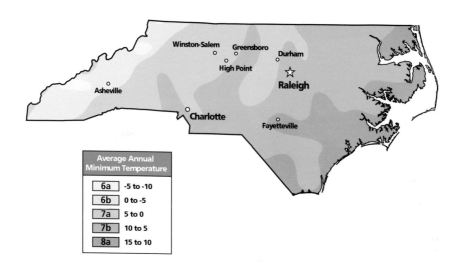

	Average Annual Minimum Temperature
6a	-5 to -10
6b	0 to -5
7a	5 to 0
7b	10 to 5
8a	15 to 10

areas when you plan your garden and choose your plants; you may even grow out-of-zone plants successfully in a warm, sheltered location.

Selecting Plants

It's important to purchase healthy plants that are free of pests and diseases. Such plants will establish quickly in your garden and won't introduce problems that may spread to other plants. You should have a good idea of what the plant is supposed to look like—the color and shape of the leaves and the habit of the plant—and then inspect the plant for signs of disease or infestation.

The majority of plants are container-grown. This is an efficient way for nurseries and greenhouses to grow plants, but when plants grow in a restricted space for too long, they can become pot bound with their roots densely encircling the inside of the pot. Avoid purchasing plants in this condition; they are often stressed and can take longer to establish. In some cases they may not establish at all. It is often possible to remove pots temporarily to look at the condition of the roots. You can check for soil-borne insects and rotten roots at the same time.

Planting Basics

The following tips apply to all plants:

- Prepare the garden before planting. Dig over the soil, pull up any weeds and make any needed amendments before you begin planting, if possible. This may be more difficult in established beds to which you want to add a single plant. The prepared area should be at least twice the size of the plant's rootball and, preferably, the expected size of the mature plant.

- Settle the soil with water. Good contact between the roots and the soil is important, but if you press the soil down too firmly, as often happens when you step on the soil, you can cause compaction, which reduces the movement of water through the soil and leaves very few air spaces. Instead, pour water in as you fill the hole with soil. The water will settle the soil evenly without allowing it to compact.

- Unwrap the roots. It is always best to remove any container before planting to give roots the chance to spread out naturally when planted. In particular, you should remove plastic containers, fiber pots, wire and burlap before planting trees. Fiber pots decompose very slowly, if at all, and wick moisture away from the plant. Synthetic burlap won't decompose, and wire can strangle the roots as they mature. The only exceptions to this rule are peat pots and pellets used to start annuals and vegetables; these decompose and can be planted with the young transplants.

Gently remove container.

Ensure proper planting depth.

Backfill with soil.

- Accommodate the rootball. If you prepared your planting spot ahead of time, your planting hole will only need to be big enough to accommodate the same depth as the rootball and twice as wide across.

- Know the mature size. Place your plants based on how big the plants will grow rather than how big they are when you plant them. Large plants should have enough room to mature without interfering with walls, roof overhangs, power lines and walkways.

- Plant at the same soil depth. Plants generally like to grow at a specific level in relation to the soil and should be planted at the same level they were growing at before you transplanted them.

- Identify your plants. Keep track of what's what in your garden by putting a tag next to your plant when you plant it, or by making an overhead drawing with plant names and locations. It is very easy for beginning gardeners to forget exactly what they planted and where they planted it.

- Water deeply and infrequently. It's better to water deeply once every week or two rather than to water lightly more often. Deep watering forces roots to grow as they search for water and helps them survive dry spells when water bans may restrict your watering regime. Always check the root zone before you water. More gardeners overwater than underwater.

Annuals

Annuals are planted new each year and are only expected to last for a single growing season. Their flowers and decorative foliage provide bright splashes of color and can fill in spaces around immature trees, shrubs and perennials.

Annuals are easy to plant and are usually sold in small packs of four or six. The roots quickly fill the space in these small packs, so the small rootball should be gently loosened before planting.

Many annuals are grown from seed and can be started directly in the garden. Some plants dislike their roots being disturbed, and these plants are often grown directly from seed or grown in peat pots or pellets to minimize root disturbance.

Winter annuals can be planted in late fall and early winter. Summer annuals can be planted in spring. Be aware of your local frost dates, as some summer annuals are quite tender.

Perennials

Perennials grow for three or more years. Many die back to the ground each fall and send up new shoots in spring, though some are evergreen. They often have a shorter period of bloom than annuals but require less care.

Settle backfilled soil with water.

Water the plant well.

Add a layer of mulch.

Many perennials benefit from being divided every few years. This keeps them growing and blooming vigorously, and in some cases controls their spread. Dividing involves digging the plant up, removing dead bits, breaking the plant into several pieces and replanting some or all of the pieces. Extra pieces can be given as gifts to family, friends and neighbors.

Trees & Shrubs

Trees and shrubs provide the bones of the garden. They are often the slowest growing plants, but usually live the longest. Characterized by leaf type, they may be deciduous or evergreen, and needled or broad-leaved.

Trees should have as little disturbed soil as possible at the bottom of the planting hole. Loose dirt settles over time and sinking even an inch can kill some trees.

Staking, sometimes recommended for newly planted trees, should only be considered for trees over 5' tall.

Pruning is more often required for shrubs than trees. It helps them maintain an attractive shape and can improve blooming. It is a good idea to take a pruning course or to hire or

Trees and shrubs are the backbone of the garden.

consult with an ISA (International Society of Arboriculture) certified arborist if you have never pruned before.

Roses

Roses are beautiful shrubs with lovely, often-fragrant blooms. Traditionally, most roses only bloomed once in the growing season, but new varieties bloom all, or almost all, summer.

Generally, roses prefer a fertile, well-prepared planting area. A rule of thumb is to prepare an area 24" across, front to back and side to side, and 24" deep. Add plenty of compost or other fertile organic matter and keep roses well watered during the growing season. Many roses are quite durable and will adapt to poorer conditions. Roses, like all shrubs, have specific pruning requirements.

Vines

Vines or climbing plants are useful for screening and shade, especially in a location too small for a tree. They may be woody or herbaceous and annual or perennial.

Roses are lovely on their own or in mixed borders.

Vines add depth to your garden structures.

Virginia Creeper provides beautiful red fall color.

Most vines need sturdy supports to grow up on. Trellises, arbors, porch railings, fences, walls, poles and trees are all possible supports. If a support is needed, ensure it's in place before you plant to avoid disturbing the roots later.

Bulbs, Corms & Tubers

These plants have fleshy underground storage organs that allow them to survive extended periods of dormancy. They are often grown for the bright splashes of color their flowers provide. They may be spring, summer, winter or fall flowering.

Hardy bulbs can be left in the ground and will flower every year, but many popular tender plants grow from bulbs, corms or tubers. These tender plants are generally lifted from the garden in fall as the foliage dies back, and are stored in a cool, frost-free location for winter, to be replanted in spring.

Herbs

Herbs may be medicinal or culinary and are often both. A few common culinary herbs are listed in this book. Even if you don't cook with herbs,

the often-fragrant foliage adds its aroma to the garden, and the plants have decorative forms, leaves and flowers.

Many herbs have pollen-producing flowers that attract butterflies, bees and hummingbirds. They also attract predatory insects. These useful insects help to manage your pest problems by feasting on problem insects such as aphids, mealy bugs and whiteflies.

Ferns, Grasses & Groundcovers

Foliage is an important consideration when choosing plants for your garden. Although many plants look spectacular in bloom, they can seem rather dull without flowers. Including a variety of plants with unique, interesting, or striking foliage can provide all the color and texture you want without the need to rely on flowers.

Ferns are ancient plants that have adapted to many different environments. The fern family is a very large group of plants with interesting foliage in a wide array of shapes and colors. Ferns do not produce flowers, but instead reproduce by spores borne in

Ornamental grasses add color, variety and texture.

structures on the undersides and margins of the foliage. Ferns are generally planted in moist, shaded gardens, but some will thrive in dry shade under the deep shade of some trees such as maples.

Ornamental grasses are becoming very popular additions to the garden. Grasses offer a variety of textures and foliage colors, and at least three seasons of interest. There is an ornamental grass for every garden situation and condition. Some grasses will thrive in any garden condition, including hot and dry to cool and wet, and in all types of soils.

North Carolina has some unique native plants.

Ornamental grasses have very few insect or disease problems. They require very little maintenance other than cutting the perennial grasses back in fall or spring.

Basically any plant that covers the ground can be used as a groundcover. Groundcovers are often spreading plants with dense growth that are used to control soil erosion, to keep weeds at bay, and to fill garden areas that are difficult to maintain. Groundcovers can be herbaceous or woody and annual or perennial.

Vines and plants that are aggressive spreaders make excellent groundcovers, but any plant with dense growth, if enough of them are planted, will serve the purpose. Space plants closer together when planting to ensure the ground is completely covered.

We have included a variety of plants grown for their foliage throughout the book. Many annuals, perennials, trees, shrubs, vines and herbs have wonderful foliage and will be an asset to your garden landscape.

Final Comments

We encourage you to visit the outstanding garden shows, county and state fairs, public and botanical gardens, arboreta and private gardens (get permission first) we have in North Carolina to see what plants grow best and if any plants catch your interest. A walk through your neighborhood is also a grand way to see what plants might do well in your own garden. Don't be afraid to ask questions.

Also don't be afraid to experiment. No matter how many books you read, trying things yourself is the best way to learn and to find out what will grow in your garden. Use the information provided as guidelines, and have fun!

Blanket Flower

Gaillardia

This native annual is sure to turn up the heat in your garden with fiery shades of yellow, red, orange and every shade and combination in between.

Growing

Blanket flower prefers **full sun**. The soil should be of **poor or average fertility**, **light**, **sandy** and **well drained**. The less water this plant receives, the better it will do. Don't cover the seeds, because they need light to germinate. They also require warm soil.

Deadhead to encourage more blooms.

Tips

Blanket flower has an informal, sprawling habit that makes it a perfect addition to a casual cottage garden or mixed border. Because it is drought tolerant, it is well suited to exposed, sunny slopes where it can help retain soil while more permanent plants grow in.

Make sure to place blanket flower in a location where it will not get watered with other plants.

Recommended

G. pulchella forms a basal rosette of leaves. The daisy-like flowers are red with yellow tips. Many cultivars and hybrids exist, including **'Arizona Sun,'** a 2005 All-American Selection winner,

G. pulchella 'Sundance Bicolor' (above)
G. pulchella cultivar (below)

bearing fiery-colored flowers earlier than most others; **'Sundance Bicolor'** bears double flowers in a combination of red, yellow and orange; and **'Torch Yellow'** bears bright yellow blossoms.

Almost every species from this genus of annuals, perennials and biennials is native to the U.S.

Features: red, orange, yellow, long-lasting flowers; habit **Height:** 12–36"
Spread: 12–24"

Butter Daisy

Melampodium

M. paludosum cultivar (above), M. paludosum (below)

The soil should be **well drained**, of **average fertility** and amended with compost. It should be kept moist until the plants are established, but allowed to dry out between waterings. This will build the plants' tolerance to drought throughout the hot summer months. Butter daisy prefers not to be fertilized too frequently.

Tips

Butter daisy is ideal for planting en masse in flowerbeds for maximum impact. They will fill and spread without becoming invasive, requiring fewer plants for a larger area. The dwarf varieties are better suited to containers and mix well with an assortment of other annuals and perennials.

Recommended

M. paludosum produces masses of starry-shaped, bright yellow flowers atop narrow, dark green leaves on short stems. The species is compact or mounding in habit. A number of cultivars are available. **'Lemon Delight'** is an exceptional dwarf cultivar; **'Medallion'** bears bright yellow flowers on 2–3' tall plants; and **'Million Gold'** is a cultivar that grows 12" tall.

This annual is a self-cleaning plant that sheds its spent flowers on a regular basis and doesn't require pinching to encourage branching. Let it be and watch it thrive.

This southern favorite is adored for its bright sunny flowers, its growth habit and its ability to tolerate extreme heat and humidity without melting down in the middle of summer.

Growing

Butter daisy prefers **full to partial sun** throughout most of North Carolina, but requires a little afternoon shade on the coast to prevent leaf scorch.

Features: bright yellow flowers; habit; drought tolerance **Height:** 10–36" **Spread:** 12–24"

Coleus

Solenostemon (Coleus)

There is a coleus for everyone. With foliage from brash yellows, oranges and reds to deep maroon and rose selections, the colors, textures and variations of coleus are almost limitless.

Growing

Most coleus prefer to grow in **light or partial shade**, but they tolerate full shade if the shade isn't too dense, or full sun if the plants are watered regularly. New sun-loving coleus selections are now available and are hardy for the intense sun of the Southeast, whereas some of the shade-loving coleus don't like any direct sunlight touching their leaves. The soil should be of **rich to average fertility, humus rich, moist** and **well drained**.

Tips

The bold, colorful foliage makes a dramatic impact when the plants are grouped together as edging plants or in beds, borders or mixed containers. Coleus can also be grown indoors or overwintered as a houseplant in a bright room.

When flower buds develop, it is best to pinch them off, because the plants tend to stretch out and become less attractive after they flower.

Recommended

S. scutellarioides (*Coleus blumei* var. *verschaffeltii*) forms a bushy mound of foliage. The leaf edges range from

S. scutellarioides cultivar (above & below)

slightly toothed to very ruffled. The leaves are usually multi-colored with shades ranging from pale greenish yellow to deep purple-black. Dozens of cultivars are available, but many cannot be started from seed. **Sunlover Series** is a sun-loving group of coleus available in wonderful color combinations.

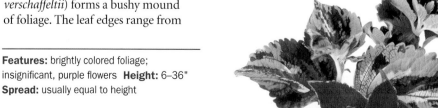

Features: brightly colored foliage; insignificant, purple flowers **Height:** 6–36"
Spread: usually equal to height

Cosmos

Cosmos

C. sulphureus (above), *C. bipinnatus* (below)

With their array of bright shades, cosmos flowers add a splash of color to any garden.

Growing

Cosmos prefer **full sun** in a **sheltered location**, out of the wind. The soil should be of **poor or average fertility** and **well drained**. These plants are drought tolerant, so too much water or fertilizer can reduce flowering. Sow seed directly into the garden in spring. Deadhead to encourage more flowering. The taller selections may need support to prevent them from falling over.

Cosmos make lovely and long-lasting additions to cut flower arrangements.

Tips

Cosmos make an attractive addition to cottage gardens, at the backs of borders and mass planted in informal beds and borders.

Recommended

C. bipinnatus is a tall plant with feathery foliage. It bears flowers in many shades of pink as well as red, purple or white. Older cultivars grow 3–6' tall, while some of the newer varieties grow 12–36" tall. Many cultivars are available, including the dwarf series called **Sonata**, bearing flowers in red, white or pink. **'Gazebo'** bears white, lavender pink and crimson flowers.

C. sulphureus (sulphur cosmos) is an erect, bushy annual with deeply lobed leaves and orange or yellowish red flowers. **'Cosmic Orange'** is an award-winning strain, producing bushy plants with large, bright orange flowers.

Features: pink, purple, red, white, yellow, orange flowers; feathery foliage **Height:** 1–6' **Spread:** 12–24"

Fan Flower
Scaevola

Fan flower's intriguing, one-sided flowers add interest to hanging baskets, containers and window boxes.

Growing
Fan flower tolerates full sun but grows well in **partial sun to light shade**. The soil should be of **average fertility, moist** and very **well drained**. Water regularly because this plant doesn't like to dry out completely. It does, however, recover quickly from wilting when watered.

Tips
Fan flower is popular for hanging baskets and containers, but it can also be used in rock gardens and along the tops of rock walls where it will trail down. This plant makes an interesting addition to mixed borders or it can be used under shrubs, where the long, trailing stems form an attractive summertime groundcover.

Recommended
S. aemula forms a mound of foliage from which trailing stems emerge. The fan-shaped flowers come in shades of bluish purple or lavender, usually with white bases. The species is rarely grown because there are many improved cultivars, including the **Outback Series**, bearing large flowers in several colors.

S. aemula (above & below)

Given the right conditions, this Australian plant will flower abundantly from April through to frost.

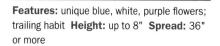

Features: unique blue, white, purple flowers; trailing habit **Height:** up to 8" **Spread:** 36" or more

Flowering Cabbage
Brassica

B. oleracea cultivar (above & below)

$\mathcal{F}$lowering cabbage has stunning, unique foliage and is wonderful in wintertime colorbeds, containers and flower boxes.

Growing
Flowering cabbage prefers **full sun** but tolerates partial shade. The soil should be **neutral to slightly alkaline,** fertile, **well drained** and **moist**. For best results, fertilize a couple of times through the winter.

Flowering cabbage can be started in trays and transplanted in fall. Many packages of seeds contain a variety of cultivars. Transplants are set out into the landscape in fall.

The plant colors brighten after a light frost or when the air temperature drops below 50° F.

Tips
Flowering cabbage is a tough, bold plant that is at home in mixed flowerbeds and in containers. It adds a punch of color in the fall and winter months.

Recommended
B. oleracea (**Acephala Group**) forms loose, erect rosettes of large, often-fringed leaves in shades of purple, red, pink or white. It grows 12–24" tall with an equal spread. The **Peacock Series** is very showy. This series has feathery, fine red or white leaves. Cooler temperatures will produce deeper tones. The **Feather Series** performs well and flowers late in the season.

When flowering cabbage bolts (sends up flowers), it is best to remove the flowers to extend the ornamental value of the plant.

Features: colorful, ornate foliage
Height: 12–24" **Spread:** 12–24"

Impatiens
Impatiens

I. walleriana (above), *I. hawkeri* (below)

Impatiens are the high-wattage darlings of the shade garden, delivering masses of flowers in a wide variety of colors.

Growing

Impatiens do best in **partial shade** or **light shade** but tolerate full shade or, if kept moist, full sun. New Guinea impatiens are the best adapted to sunny locations. The soil should be **fertile, humus rich, moist** and **well drained**.

Tips

Impatiens are known for their ability to grow and flower profusely, even in shade. Mass plant them in beds under trees, along shady fences and walls or in porch planters. They also look lovely in hanging baskets. New Guinea impatiens are grown as much for their variegated leaves as for their flowers.

Recommended

I. hawkeri (New Guinea hybrids, New Guinea impatiens) flowers in shades of red, orange, pink, purple or white. The foliage is often variegated with a yellow stripe down the center of each leaf. Many cultivars are available in various flower and foliage colors.

I. walleriana (impatiens, busy Lizzie) flowers in shades of purple, red, burgundy, pink, yellow, salmon, orange, apricot or white and can be bicolored. Dozens of cultivars are available.

New impatiens varieties are introduced every year, expanding the selection of sizes, forms and colors.

Features: flowers in shades of purple, red, burgundy, pink, yellow, salmon, orange, apricot, white, bicolored; flowers well in shade
Height: 6–36" **Spread:** 12–24"

Lantana

Lantana

L. camara cultivar (above), *L. camara* 'Radiation' (below)

These low-maintenance plants, with their stunning flowers, thrive in hot weather and won't suffer if you forget to water them.

Growing

Lantana grows best in **full sun** but tolerates partial shade. The soil should be **fertile, moist** and **well drained**. Plants are heat and drought tolerant. Cuttings can be taken in late summer and grown indoors for the winter so you will have plants the following summer. Occasionally, in the right spot, lantana will become a perennial.

Tips

Lantana is a tender shrub that is grown as an annual. It makes an attractive addition to beds and borders as well as in mixed containers and hanging baskets.

Recommended

L. camara is a bushy plant that bears round clusters of flowers in a variety of colors. The flowers often change color as they mature, giving flower clusters a striking, multi-colored appearance. Good examples of this are **'Feston Rose,'** which has flowers that open yellow and mature to bright pink, and LUCKY RED HOT IMPROVED which was rated best lantana at the JC Raulston Arboretum in 2004. **'Miss Huff'** is reliably perennial in zone 7, bearing showy orange, yellow or pink flowers, and **'Radiation'** bears flowers that open yellow and mature to red.

These shrubby annuals grow quickly and make a stunning addition to mixed planters, combining well with geraniums and other heat-tolerant annuals.

Features: flowers in stunning colors of yellow, orange, pink, purple, red, white, often in combination **Height:** 18–24" **Spread:** up to 4'

Madagascar Periwinkle

Catharanthus

Madagascar periwinkle is a forgiving annual, tolerant of dry spells, searing sun and city pollution. It exhibits grace under all sorts of pressure.

Growing

Madagascar periwinkle prefers **full sun** but tolerates partial shade. Any **well-drained** soil is fine. This plant tolerates pollution and drought but prefers to be **watered regularly**. It doesn't like to be too wet or too cold. Avoid planting this annual until the soil has warmed because it may fail to thrive if planted in cold or wet soil.

Tips

Madagascar periwinkle does well in the sunniest, warmest part of the garden. Plant it in a bed along an exposed driveway or against a south-facing wall. It can also be used in hanging baskets, in containers and as a temporary groundcover.

C. roseus (above & below)

Recommended

C. roseus (*Vinca rosea*) forms a mound of strong stems. The flowers are pink, red or white, often with contrasting centers. Many cultivars are available, including the **Pacifica Series**, bearing flowers in lilac, pale pink or white, and the **Tropicana Series,** which is early blooming and has very large, rounded flowers.

One of the best annuals to use in front of homes on busy streets, Madagascar periwinkle will bloom happily despite exposure to exhaust fumes and dust.

Features: attractive foliage; flowers in shades of red, rose, pink, mauve, white, often with contrasting centers; durable plants **Height:** 6–24" **Spread:** usually equal to or greater than height

Mexican Sunflower
Tithonia

T. rotundifolia (above & below)

Cover seeds lightly because they germinate more evenly and quickly when exposed to some light. Mexican sunflower needs little water or care; however, it will bloom more profusely if it is deadheaded regularly.

Tips
Mexican sunflower is heat resistant, so it is ideal for growing in a sunny, warm spot. The plants are tall and break easily if exposed to too much wind; grow along a wall or fence to provide shelter and stability. These annuals are coarse in appearance and are well suited to the back of a border where they can provide a good backdrop to a bed of shorter annuals.

Recommended
T. rotundifolia is a vigorous, bushy plant. Vibrant orange flowers are produced. '**Goldfinger**' is taller than the species, growing to 6', and bears large, orange flowers. '**Fiesta del Sol**' was the first dwarf cultivar from this group and received the All-American Selection designation in 1968. It grows 3' tall and bears deep orange flowers. '**Torch**' has bright red-orange flowers.

The stems of this annual are hollow, so be careful when cutting them to prevent damage.

For that 'hot' look in the garden, Mexican sunflower is one of the best plants you can grow. It is also a perfect landing pad for butterflies from late summer into fall.

Growing
This annual grows best in **full sun**. The soil should be of **average to poor fertility, moist** and **well drained**.

Features: orange, red-orange, yellow-orange flowers; tolerance to heat and humidity
Height: 3–6' **Spread:** 2–2½'

Moss Rose
Portulaca

For a brilliant show in the hottest, driest, most neglected area of the garden, you can't go wrong with moss rose.

Growing

Moss rose requires **full sun**. The soil should be of **poor fertility, sandy** and **well drained**. To ensure that you will have plants where you want them, start seeds indoors. If you sow directly outdoors, the tiny seeds may get washed away by rain, and the plants will pop up in unexpected places. Moss rose also self-seeds and can provide a colorful show from year to year.

Tips

Moss rose grows well under the eaves of a house or in a dry, rocky, exposed area. It also makes a great addition to a hanging basket on a sunny front porch. Remember to water it occasionally. As long as the location is sunny, this plant will do well with minimal care.

Recommended

P. x *grandiflora* (moss rose) forms a bushy mound of succulent foliage. It bears delicate, papery, rose-like flowers profusely all summer. Many cultivars are available, including those with flowers that stay open on cloudy days.

P. x *grandiflora* (above & below)

P. oleracea (ornamental purslane) produces succulent foliage, wider than that of *P.* x *grandiflora*, and single or double, neon-bright yellow flowers.

The species oleracea *is Latin for 'vegetables,' referring to this plant's common use as a salad green.*

Features: colorful, drought-resistant summer flowers in shades of red, pink, yellow, white, purple, orange, peach **Height:** 4–8"
Spread: 6–12" or wider

Pansy
Viola

V. x wittrockiana (above), *V. tricolor* (below)

Growing

Pansies prefer **full sun** but tolerate partial shade. The soil should be **fertile, moist** and **well drained**. Pansies do best in cool weather so plant them in late September through October. It is the heat of summer that kills them, so planting in the spring is not recommended.

Tips

Pansies can be used in beds and borders for winter color or mixed with spring-flowering bulbs. They can also be grown in containers. With the varied color combinations available, pansies complement almost every other type of bedding plant.

Recommended

V. tricolor (Johnny jump up) is a perennial grown as an annual but will reseed. It bears flowers in shades of purple, lavender blue, white or yellow, with dark purple upper petals. The lower petals are usually streaked with dark purple. Many cultivars exist with larger flowers in various colors above heart-shaped leaves.

V. x *wittrockiana* is available in every size imaginable. It bears a wide variety of solid, patterned, bicolored or multi-colored flowers with face-like markings. The foliage is bright green and lightly scalloped along the edges.

Pansies are one of the most popular annuals available, and for good reason. They are planted in early fall, often blooming off and on throughout the winter months, and put on quite the show in spring. Late-blooming forms can also be planted in late winter.

Owing to the long growing season, pansies must be continuously fertilized through the winter.

Features: blue, purple, red, orange, yellow, pink, white, multi-colored flowers
Height: 3–10" **Spread:** 6–12"

Persian Shield
Strobilanthes

Iridescent foliage in metallic shades of purple, bronze, silver and pink add a bright touch to any annual planting.

Growing

Persian shield grows well in **full sun** or **partial shade**. The soil should be **average to fertile, light** and very **well drained**. Pinch the growing tips to encourage bushy growth. Cuttings can be started in late summer and overwintered indoors.

Tips

The colorful foliage provides a dramatic background in annual or mixed beds and borders and in container plantings. Combine Persian shield with plants that have yellow, white, red or purple flowers for stunning contrast.

Recommended

S. dyerianus forms a mound of silver- or purple-flushed foliage with contrasting dark green, bronze or purple veins and margins. Plants may produce spikes of blue flowers in early fall.

S. dyerianus (above & below)

The common name arose because this plant's foliage was thought to resemble the colorful shields carried by soldiers in ancient Persia.

Features: decorative foliage; blue flowers
Height: 18–36" **Spread:** 24–36" or more

Petunia

Petunia

Grandiflora type (above), Multiflora type (below)

For speedy growth, prolific blooming, ease of care and a huge variety of selections, petunias are hard to beat.

Growing

Petunias prefer **full sun**. The soil should be of **average to rich fertility, light, sandy** and **well drained**. Pinch halfway back in mid-summer to keep plants bushy and to encourage new growth and flowers.

Tips

Use petunias in beds, borders, containers and hanging baskets.

Recommended

P. x *hybrida* is a large group of popular, sun-loving annuals that fall into three categories: **grandifloras** have the largest flowers in the widest range of colors, but they can be damaged by rain; **multifloras** bear more flowers that are smaller and less easily damaged by heavy rain; and **millifloras** have the smallest flowers in the narrowest range of colors, but this type is the most prolific and is least likely to be damaged by heavy rain. Cultivars of all types are available and new selections are made available almost every year. The **Wave Series** is perhaps the most recognizable.

Features: flowers in every color, solid, bicolored, multi-colored; versatile plants
Height: 6–18" **Spread:** 12–24" or more

Trailing Petunia
Calibrachoa

C. Million Bells Series 'Terracotta' (above), C. Million Bells Series 'Trailing Pink' (below)

*T*railing petunias are charming, and given the right conditions, will bloom continually during the growing season.

Growing
Trailing petunias prefer **full sun**. The soil should be **fertile, moist** and **well drained**. Although they prefer to be watered regularly, trailing petunias are fairly drought resistant once established.

Tips
Popular for containers and hanging baskets, trailing petunias are also attractive in beds and borders. They grow all summer and need plenty of room to spread or they will overtake other flowers. Pinch back to keep the plants compact.

Recommended
Calibrachoa **hybrids** have a dense, trailing habit. They bear small flowers that are reminiscent of tiny petunia blossoms. The **Superbells** and **Million Bells Series** are noted for superior disease resistance and a wide range of uniquely colored flowers.

Trailing petunias bloom well into autumn; they become hardier over summer and as the weather cools.

Features: pink, purple, yellow, red-orange, white, blue flowers; trailing habit
Height: 6–12" **Spread:** up to 24"

Zinnia
Zinnia

Z. x elegans 'Super Giants' (above), *Z. x elegans* cultivars (below)

Zinnias are popular in gardens and flower arrangements, adding much needed color to the late-summer and fall garden.

Growing
Zinnias grow best in **full sun.** The soil should be **fertile, rich in organic matter, moist** and **well drained**. Allow air to circulate between the plants to discourage mildew. To avoid disturbing the roots when transplanting seedlings, start seeds in individual peat pots. Deadhead to prolong blooming and to keep plants looking neat.

Tips
Zinnias are useful in beds, borders, containers and cutting gardens. The dwarf selections can be used as edging plants. These plants provide wonderful summer to fall color.

Recommended
Z. angustifolia (spreading zinnia, narrow-leaf zinnia) is a low, mounding, mildew-resistant plant that bears yellow, orange or white flowers. It grows to about 8" tall. Cultivars are available, including the **Profusion Series**, bearing flowers in shades of pink, orange or white.

Z. x *elegans* is a bushy, upright plant with daisy-like flowers in a variety of forms. Heights vary from 6–36". Many cultivars are available.

Z. haageana (Mexican zinnia) is a bushy plant with narrow leaves that bears bright bicolored or tricolored, daisy-like flowers in shades of orange, red, yellow, maroon, brown or gold. Plants grow 12–24" tall. Cultivars are available.

Features: bushy plants; flowers in shades of red, yellow, green, purple, orange, pink, white, maroon, brown, gold, some are bicolored or tricolored **Height:** 6–36" **Spread:** 12–24"

Anise Hyssop
Agastache

This perennial is a favorite not only with southern gardeners but also with hummingbirds and butterflies.

Growing

Anise hyssop requires **full sun** or **partial shade**. The soil should be **well drained** and **fertile**. Dead-heading will encourage the plants to re-bloom.

Tips

Anise hyssop is well suited to perennial borders as an ornamental, or in herb gardens for culinary use. It is often used in cottage-garden settings and in garden designs meant to attract butterflies, hummingbirds and pollinating insects.

Recommended

A. cana (Texas hummingbird mint, mosquito plant, wild hyssop) is an erect-growing plant with bubblegum- or camphor-scented leaves and flowers. It bears loose spikes of dark pink to pink-purple flowers. A few cultivars are available.

A. foeniculum (anise hyssop) produces anise- or licorice-scented, roughly textured leaves with downy, light green undersides, and dense clusters of lilac blue flowers. It grows quite tall compared to its mature width. Cultivars are available but often the species is more commonly found.

A. foeniculum cultivars (above)
A. foeniculum (below)

A. rugosa (wrinkled giant hyssop, Korean hummingbird mint) has aromatic, toothed leaves in green with a hint of purple, and short flower spikes that are violet to pinkish purple. This species is cold hardy. Cultivars are available in more compact forms and colors.

A. rupestris (licorice mint, sunset hyssop) is smaller than its counterparts and bears gray-green fine leaves and orange flower spikes. The foliage is extremely fragrant.

Features: aromatic foliage; pink, purple, purplish blue, orange flowers; tolerance to wet soil **Height:** 1½–5' **Spread:** 1–3' **Hardiness:** zones 5–9

Aster

Aster (Symphyotrichum)

A. *novae-angliae* (above), A. *novi-belgii* (below)

Asters are among the final plants to bloom before first frost; their purples and pinks contrast with the yellow-flowered perennials common in the late-summer and fall garden.

Growing

Asters prefer **full sun** but tolerate partial shade. The soil should be **fertile, moist** and **well drained**. Pinch or shear these plants back in early summer to promote dense growth and to reduce disease problems.

Tips

Use asters in the middle of borders and in cottage gardens, or naturalize them in wild gardens.

Recommended

Some *Aster* species have recently been reclassified under the genus *Symphyotrichum*. You may see both names at garden centers. Here are just a few of the most popular species.

A. carolinianus (climbing aster) is an unusual climber with yellow-centered, pink to purplish blue fall flowers. It can grow to 12' tall. *A. divaricatus* (white wood aster) tolerates more shade than other species, bearing white flowers that change to pink. *A. x frikartii* (frikart aster) is an upright perennial with light to dark violet-blue flowers that emerge in late summer. *A. grandiflorus* (great aster) bears large, single, deep violet flowers on tall, slender stems.

A. novae-angliae (Michaelmas daisy, New England aster) is a clump-forming species that bears yellow-centered, purple flowers, and *A. novi-belgii* (Michaelmas daisy, New York aster) also produces purple flowers atop an upright form. Cultivars are available for all these selections.

Features: late-summer to mid-autumn flowers in shades of red, white, blue, purple, pink, often with yellow centers **Height:** 2–12' **Spread:** 2–4' **Hardiness:** zones 3–8

Baptisia
Baptisia

B. australis (above & below)

Spikes of bright blue, yellow or white flowers in early summer and attractive green foliage make baptisia a worthy addition, even if it does take up a sizable amount of garden real estate.

Growing

Baptisia prefers **full sun** but tolerates partial shade, though too much shade causes lank growth that flops over easily. The soil should be of **poor to average fertility, sandy** and **well drained**.

Tips

Baptisia can be used in an informal border or in a cottage garden. It is an attractive addition for a naturalized planting, on a slope, or in any sunny, well-drained spot.

Recommended

B. alba (white wild indigo) is an erect perennial with a bushy growth habit. It bears tall spikes of white flowers that are sometimes marked with purple. This species grows 2–4' tall and 2' wide.

B. australis (false blue indigo) is an upright or somewhat spreading, clump-forming plant that bears spikes of purple-blue flowers in early summer.

B. 'Carolina Moonlight' grows 4–4½' tall and 3–4' wide. Clusters of soft yellow flowers are borne in late spring. The foliage turns to silvery blue during the hottest period of summer.

B. 'Purple Smoke' grows 4½' tall, bearing violet flowers with dark purple centers.

Features: late-spring or early-summer flowers in yellow, blue, purple, white; habit; foliage
Height: 2–4½' **Spread:** 2–4'
Hardiness: zones 3–9

Bear's Breeches
Acanthus

A. spinosus (above & below)

This dramatic perennial is anything but subtle; it exudes a personality shared by few others.

Growing

Bear's breeches will grow in **partial sun to full shade** in just about any **well-drained** soil. The soil should be of **average to poor fertility** and **moist**. The spreading root system is inclined to become aggressive if the soil is too rich. Be sure to keep the plants well watered if planted during hot, dry weather to help them become established.

Bear's breeches are drought tolerant but do best if given an occasional soaking when the weather is excessively hot with little rainfall.

Tips

Bear's breeches are bold and dramatic plants that form large clumps. They work well as the central planting in an island bed or at the back of a border. They are often grown just for the dramatic foliage.

Recommended

*A. **mollis*** (common bear's breeches) forms a large clump of lobed foliage. It is the classic leaf on Corinthian columns. Tall spikes of white and purple bicolored flowers are borne in late spring to summer.

*A. **spinosus*** (spiny bear's breeches) forms a clump of silvery, very spiny foliage. It is more tolerant of humid conditions and winter cold and is less aggressive than *A. mollis*. The white flowers with purple to rose-purple bracts are borne from early spring to mid-summer.

Acanthus is derived from the Greek word akanthos (thorny), a reference to the often spiny nature of these plants. It is one of the oldest named perennials.

Features: ornate, bold foliage; tall, white and purple bicolored flower spikes **Height:** 4–5' **Spread:** 3–4' **Hardiness:** zones 5–9

Black-Eyed Susan
Rudbeckia

R. fulgida var. *sullivantii* 'Goldsturm' with coneflower (above), *R. nitida* 'Herbstsonne' (below)

lack-eyed Susan is a tough, low-maintenance, long-lived perennial. Plant it wherever you want a casual look. It looks great planted in drifts.

Growing
Black-eyed Susan grows well in **full sun** or **partial shade**. The soil should be of **average fertility** and **well drained**. Several *Rudbeckia* species are touted as 'claybusters' because of their tolerance of fairly heavy clay soils. Established plants are drought tolerant but regular watering is best. Divide in spring or fall, every three to five years.

Tips
Include these native plants in wildflower and natural gardens, beds and borders.

Features: bright flowers in yellow, orange, red, with centers typically brown or green; attractive foliage; easy to grow
Height: 2–10'   **Spread:** 1½ –4'
Hardiness: zones 3–8

Recommended
*R. **fulgida*** is an upright, native, spreading plant bearing orange-yellow flowers with brown centers. The species grows 3' tall and 2' wide. **Var.** *sullivantii* **'Goldsturm'** bears large, bright, golden yellow flowers. This variety is slightly smaller in size.

*R. **laciniata*** (cutleaf coneflower) forms a large, open clump. The yellow flowers have green centers. This species can grow up to 10' tall and 4' wide, but less aggressive cultivars are available.

*R. **nitida*** is an upright, spreading plant 3–6' tall and 2–3' in spread. The yellow flowers have green centers. **'Herbstsonne'** ('Autumn Sun') has bright golden yellow flowers.

Blue Star Flower

Amsonia

A. hubrichtii (above & below)

Perennials are not known for spectacular fall foliage color, but blue star flower breaks the mold with its spectacular display of stunning, golden yellow, autumn hues.

Growing

Blue star flower grows well in **full sun, partial shade** or **light shade**. The soil should be of **average fertility, moist** and **well drained**. Plants are drought tolerant once established. Divide the plant in spring to propagate more plants.

Tips

These pretty plants have a billowy appearance. Plant in groups of three to five to achieve the most dramatic results.

Recommended

A. ciliata (downy blue star) produces narrow, linear leaves and rich sky blue flowers. This native species can grow 12–36" in height and 12" in spread.

A. hubrichtii forms a clump of arching stems and thread-like, bright green leaves. Clusters of small, light blue, star-shaped flowers are produced in spring. This is followed by stunning, golden yellow, fall color. This species grows 3' tall and wide.

A. tabernaemontana (blue star flower) produces willow-like, dark green leaves and deep blue flowers. The species grows 2' tall and 18" wide. Cultivars are available with compact forms and showy, purple blooms.

Features: spring through summer flowers in blue; habit; foliage **Height:** 12–36" **Spread:** 12–36" **Hardiness:** zones 4–9

Butterfly Weed

Asclepias

A. tuberosa (above & below)

Native to North America, butterfly weeds are a major food source for the monarch butterfly and will attract butterflies to your garden.

Growing

Butterfly weeds prefer **full sun**. The soil should be **fertile, moist** and **well drained**, though *A. tuberosa* is drought tolerant.

To propagate, remove the seedlings that sprout up around the base of these plants. The deep taproot makes division very difficult.

Deadhead to encourage a second blooming.

Be careful not to pick off or destroy the green-and-black striped caterpillars feeding on these plants, as they will eventually turn into beautiful monarch butterflies.

Tips

Use *A. tuberosa* in meadow plantings and borders, on dry banks, in neglected areas and in wildflower, cottage and butterfly gardens. Butterfly weeds are slow to start in spring.

Place a marker beside each plant in fall so you won't forget the plant is there and inadvertently dig it up.

Recommended

*A. **tuberosa*** (butterfly weed) forms a clump of upright, leafy stems. It bears clusters of orange flowers from mid-summer to early fall. A variety of cultivars exist, bearing flowers in shades of scarlet, gold, orange, pink, white, purple or bicolored.

Features: orange, yellow, white, red, pink, light purple, bicolored flowers; form **Height:** 18–36" **Spread:** 12–24" **Hardiness:** zones 3–9

Chrysanthemum

Chrysanthemum

C. hybrids (above & below)

Perk up your fall garden with a bright display of fall 'mums' and their masses of colorful flowers.

Growing

Chrysanthemums grow best in **full sun**. The soil should be **fertile, moist** and **well drained**. Plant early in the growing season to increase their chances of surviving winter. Pinch plants back from spring through mid-summer to encourage bushy growth and increase flower production.

Divide plants every two or three years to ensure vigorous growth.

Tips

Chrysanthemums provide a blaze of color in the fall garden that lasts until the first hard frost. In groups, or as specimen plants, they can be included in borders, in planters or in plantings close to the house.

Recommended

C. **hybrids** are a diverse group of plant series with varied hardiness. *C.* **'Mei-Kyo'** is a vigorous grower, producing deep pink flowers in mid- to late October. The **Prophet Series** includes **'Christine,'** with deep salmon pink flowers, and **'Raquel'** with bright red flowers.

C. **maximum** (shasta daisy) is a popular, tall-growing species with white petals surrounding gold centers. It grows 2–4' in height. The cultivars are longer blooming and share improved qualities over and above the species. **'Becky'** will bloom for weeks if deadheaded.

C. **pacificum** (silver and gold chrysanthemum) is a low-growing perennial with dark green leaves with silvery undersides. It bears small, button-like, gold flowers in late fall. Cultivars are available with pink flowers.

Features: late-summer or fall flowers in every color and combination except blue
Height: 12"–4' **Spread:** 2–4'
Hardiness: zones 5–9

Columbine
Aquilegia

Delicate and beautiful columbines add a touch of simple elegance to any garden. Blooming from early spring through to summer, these long-lasting flowers herald the passing of cold weather and the arrival of hummingbirds.

Growing

Columbines grow well in **light sun to partial shade**. They prefer soil that is **fertile, moist** and **well drained** but adapt to most soil conditions. Division is not required but can be done to propagate desirable plants. Divided plants may take a while to recover because columbines dislike having their roots disturbed.

Tips

Use columbines in rock gardens, formal or casual borders and naturalized or woodland gardens. Place them where other plants can fill in to hide the foliage as the columbines may die back over the summer.

Recommended

A. alpina (alpine columbine) grows 2–3' tall and 1' wide, bearing nodding, bright blue flowers.

A. canadensis (wild columbine) bears yellow flowers with red outer spurs.

A. x hybrida (hybrid columbine) forms mounds of delicate foliage and has exceptional flowers.

A. *vulgaris* 'Nora Barlow' (above)
A. x *hybrida* 'McKana Giants' (below)

Many hybrids have been developed with showy flowers in a wide range of colors.

A. vulgaris (European columbine) has been used to develop many hybrids and cultivars with flowers in a variety of colors and forms, including double-flowered cultivars such as **'Nora Barlow'** that look like frilly dahlias.

Features: red, yellow, pink, purple, blue, white, spring flowers, color of spurs often differs from that of the petals; attractive foliage **Height:** 18–36" **Spread:** 12–24" **Hardiness:** zones 3–8

Coneflower

Echinacea

E. purpurea with black-eyed Susan (above)
E. purpurea (below)

Divide every four years or so in spring or fall.

Deadhead early in the season to prolong flowering. Later you may wish to leave the flowerheads in place to self-seed and to provide winter interest. Pinch plants back or thin out the stems in early summer to encourage bushy growth that will be less prone to mildew.

Tips

Use coneflowers in meadow gardens and informal borders, either in groups or as single specimens. The dry flowerheads make an interesting feature in fall and winter gardens.

Recommended

E. purpurea (coneflower, purple coneflower) is an upright plant that bears purple flowers with orangy centers. Cultivars are available, including selections with white or pink flowers. **'Kim's Knee High'** is a dwarf selection with bright pink, upturned flowers. Some new hybrids offer an expanded color range of orange or yellow flowers.

Coneflower is a visual delight with its mauve petals offset by a spiky, often-fragrant, orange center. New releases offer orange, yellow, or white petals with contrasting centers.

Growing

Coneflower grows well in **full sun** or very **light shade**. It tolerates any well-drained soil but prefers an **average to rich** soil. The thick taproots make this plant drought resistant, but it prefers to have regular water.

Coneflower attracts wildlife to the garden, providing pollen, nectar and seeds to various hungry visitors.

Features: mid-summer to fall purple, pink, yellow, orange, white flowers with rusty orange centers; persistent seedheads **Height:** 2–5' **Spread:** 12–24" **Hardiness:** zones 3–8

Coral Bells
Heuchera

From soft, yellow-greens and oranges to midnight purples and silvery, dappled maroons, coral bells offer a great variety of foliage options for a perennial garden with partial shade.

Growing

Coral bells grow best in **light or partial shade**. The foliage colors can bleach out in full sun, and plants grow leggy in full shade. The soil should be of **average to rich fertility, humus rich, neutral to alkaline, moist** and **well drained. Good air circulation** is essential. Deadhead to prolong the bloom. Every two or three years, coral bells should be dug up and the oldest, woodiest roots and stems should be removed. Divide the plants at this time, if desired, then replant with the crown at or just above soil level.

Tips

Use coral bells as edging plants, in clusters and woodland gardens, or as groundcovers in low-traffic areas. Combine different foliage types for an interesting display.

Recommended

There are dozens of beautiful species, cultivars and hybrids available with almost limitless variations of foliage markings and colors. *H. americana* (alum root) is a popular native species that grows 1–2' tall and wide. It bears

H. americana 'Plum Pudding' (above)
H. sanguinea (below)

green and white mottled foliage and 3' tall, greenish white flowers. A vast array of selections is available in varied colors and forms. See your local garden center or a mail-order catalog to discover what is available.

Features: very decorative foliage; spring or summer flowers in shades of red, pink, white, yellow, purple **Height:** 1–4' **Spread:** 6–24"
Hardiness: zones 3–9

Daylily
Hemerocallis

'Dewey Roquemore' (above), 'Bonanza' (below)

The daylily's adaptability and durability combined with its variety in color, blooming period, size and texture explain this sun-loving perennial's popularity.

Growing

Daylilies grow in any light from **full sun to shade**. The deeper the shade, the fewer flowers will be produced. The soil should be **fertile, moist** and **well drained,** but these plants adapt to most conditions and are hard to kill once established.

Divide every two or three years to keep plants vigorous and to propagate them. They can, however, be left indefinitely without dividing. Deadhead to prolong the blooming period. Be careful when deadheading purple-flowered daylilies because the sap can stain fingers and clothes.

Tips

Plant daylilies alone, or group them in borders, on banks and in ditches to control erosion. They can be naturalized in woodland or meadow gardens. Small varieties are also nice in planters.

Recommended

Daylilies come in an almost infinite number of forms, sizes and colors in a range of species, cultivars and hybrids. Visit your local garden center or daylily grower to find out what's available and most suitable for your garden.

Features: spring and summer flowers in every color, except true blue and pure white; strap-like foliage **Height:** 1–4' **Spread:** 1–4' **Hardiness:** zones 2–8

Gaura

Gaura

Pink and white flowers float high above the tall slender stems, resembling butterflies whirling in the sun.

Growing

Gaura prefers a location in **full sun** but tolerates partial shade. The soil should be **fertile, moist** and **well drained**. Gaura is drought tolerant once established. Division is difficult because of the deep taproot that is formed.

In order to keep this plant flowering right up until the end of the season, it is important to deadhead. Remove the spent flower spikes as they fade to promote more blossoms, to prevent excessive self-seeding and to keep the plant tidy.

Tips

Gaura makes a good addition for borders. Its color and appearance have a softening effect on brighter colors. Although it bears few flowers at a time, it blooms for the entire summer.

Recommended

*G. **lindheimeri*** (white gaura) is a clump-forming plant. It bears clusters of star-shaped white flowers that arise from pink flower buds. The flowers fade back to pink with age. **'Siskiyou Pink'** is a shorter variety, bearing bright pink flowers, and its foliage

G. *lindheimeri* (above)
G. *lindheimeri* 'Siskiyou Pink' (below)

is marked with reddish purple. **'Whirling Butterflies'** grows 36" tall and tends to have more flowers in bloom at a time.

There are about 20 species of Gaura, *and they are all native to North America.*

Features: delicate pink or white flowers; habit **Height:** 2–4' **Spread:** 24–36" **Hardiness:** zones 6–9

Hellebore
Helleborus

H. orientalis cultivar (above), *H. foetidus* (below)

These beautiful, winter-blooming, evergreen groundcover plants are among the earliest harbingers of the coming spring, providing the welcome sight of flowers long before most other plants have even started to sprout.

Growing

Hellebores prefer **light, dappled shade** and a **sheltered location** but tolerate some direct sun if the soil stays evenly moist. The soil should be **fertile, humus rich, neutral, moist** and **well drained**. Mulch plants in winter if they are in an exposed location.

Tips

Use these plants in a sheltered border or rock garden, or naturalize in a woodland garden.

Recommended

H. foetidus (bear's-foot hellebore) grows 2½' tall and wide. It bears dark green leaves and clusters of light green flowers with purplish red edges. Cultivars are available that are larger in size and have varied flower colors.

H. x *hybridus* grows about 18" tall, with an equal spread. Plants should remain evergreen, and they bloom in a wide range of colors. Some cultivars have deep-colored flowers, double flowers, spotted flowers or picotee flowers (with differently colored petal margins).

H. orientalis (lenten rose) is a clump-forming, evergreen perennial. It grows 12–24" tall, with an equal spread. It bears purple to white or greenish flowers that turn pink as they mature in mid- or late spring.

Features: late-winter to mid-spring flowers in white, green, pink, purple, yellow
Height: 12–30" **Spread:** 12–30"
Hardiness: zones 5–9

Hosta

Hosta

Breeders are always looking for new variations in hosta foliage. Swirls, stripes, puckers and ribs enhance the broad leaves' various sizes, shapes and colors.

Growing

Hostas prefer **light or partial shade** but will grow in full shade. Morning sun is preferable to afternoon sun in partial shade situations, though some hostas can take more sunlight if given plenty of moisture. The soil should be **fertile, moist** and **well drained** but most soils are tolerated. Hostas are fairly drought tolerant, especially if given a mulch to help them retain moisture. Division is not required but can be done every few years in spring or summer to propagate new plants.

H. sieboldiana 'Elegans' (above)

Tips

Hostas make wonderful woodland plants and look very attractive when combined with ferns and other fine-textured plants. Hostas are also good plants for a mixed border, particularly when used to hide the ugly, leggy, lower stems and branches of some shrubs. Hostas' dense growth and thick, shade-providing leaves allow them to suppress weeds.

Recommended

Hostas have been experiencing a great deal of crossbreeding and hybridizing, resulting in hundreds of cultivars. Visit your local garden center or get a mail-order catalog to find out what's available.

Some gardeners think the flowers clash with the foliage, and they remove the flower stems when they first emerge. If you find the flowers unattractive, removing them won't harm the plant.

Also called: plantain lily, funkia
Features: bold, decorative foliage; summer and fall flowers in white, purple **Height:** 4–36" **Spread:** 6"–6'
Hardiness: zones 3–8

Japanese Anemone
Anemone

A. x hybrida (above & below)

As the rest of the garden begins to fade in late summer, Japanese anemone is just beginning its fall show. The white and pink flowers are a welcome sight in the fall garden that is usually dominated by yellow and orange.

Growing

Japanese anemone prefers **partial or light shade**. The soil should be of **average to high fertility, humus rich** and **moist**. Allow the soil to dry out when plants are dormant. Mulch the first winter to allow plants to become established.

Deadheading keeps the plants tidy but does not prolong the blooming period.

Tips

Japanese anemones make a beautiful addition for fall interest in lightly shaded borders, woodland gardens and cottage gardens. They also look great when planted in front of red brick or wood siding, particularly natural or weathered, unpainted wood.

Recommended

A. huphensis **var.** *japonica* (Japanese anemone) is an erect perennial with long stems covered in dark green leaves and topped with creamy pink flowers from mid-summer to fall. Many cultivars are available with darker flowers and varied sizes.

A. **x** *hybrida* is an upright plant with a suckering habit. Hybrids can reach 4–5' heights and indefinite spreads. Flowers in shades of pink or white are produced in late summer and early fall. Many selections are available.

The name anemone (a-nem-o-nee) comes from the Greek word anemos *(wind), referring to the windswept mountainside habitat of some species.*

Features: late summer to fall flowers in various shades of pink or white; some with double flowers; attractive foliage **Height:** 2–5' **Spread:** 2' or more **Hardiness:** zones 4–9

Lungwort
Pulmonaria

P. saccharata (above & below)

The wide array of lungworts have highly attractive foliage that ranges in color from apple green to silver-spotted and olive to dark emerald.

Growing

Lungworts prefer **partial to full shade.** The soil should be **fertile, humus rich, moist** and **well drained.** Rot can occur in very wet soil.

Divide in late spring, after flowering, or in fall. Provide the newly planted divisions with a lot of water to help them re-establish.

Tips

Lungworts make useful and attractive groundcovers for shady borders, woodland gardens and pond and stream edges.

Recommended

P. longifolia (long-leaved lungwort) forms a dense clump of long, narrow, white-spotted, green leaves and bears clusters of blue flowers. This species grows 8–12" tall and 18" wide. Cultivars with deep blue blossoms are available.

P. saccharata (Bethlehem sage) forms a compact clump of large, white-spotted, evergreen leaves and purple, red or white flowers. The species grows 12–18" tall and up to 24" wide. Many cultivars are available with pink or white flowers.

This plant has more than 20 common names known all over the world. Many are biblical references, such as Abraham, Isaac and Jacob; Adam and Eve; Children of Israel; and Virgin Mary.

Features: decorative, mottled foliage; blue, red, pink, white spring flowers **Height:** 8–18" **Spread:** 18–24" **Hardiness:** zones 3–8

Peony
Paeonia

P. *lactiflora* cultivars (above & below)

be well prepared before the plants are introduced. Peonies like **fertile, humus-rich, moist, well-drained** soil to which a lot of compost has been added. Mulch is not necessary as peonies like winter's cold. Too much fertilizer, particularly nitrogen, causes floppy growth and retards blooming. Deadhead to keep plants looking tidy.

Tips

These wonderful plants look great in a border combined with other early bloomers. The emerging foliage of the peonies will begin to show in late winter. Avoid planting peonies under trees where they will have to compete for moisture and nutrients.

Planting depth determines whether a peony will flower. Tubers planted too deeply will not flower. The buds or eyes on the tuber should be barely below the soil surface.

Recommended

There are hundreds of peonies available. Cultivars come in a wide range of colors, may have single or double flowers, and may or may not be fragrant. It's best to grow heat-tolerant varieties that won't 'melt-down' in the summer heat. Visit your local garden center to see what is available.

From the simple, single flowers to the extravagant doubles, it's easy to become mesmerized with these voluptuous plants. Once the fleeting, but magnificent, flower display is done, the foliage remains stellar throughout the growing season.

Growing

Peonies prefer **full sun** but tolerate some shade. The planting site should

Features: white, cream, yellow, pink, red, purple spring flowers; attractive foliage
Height: 24–32" **Spread:** 24–32"
Hardiness: zones 2–8

Perennial Salvia

Salvia

S. hybrid (above), S. azurea (below)

The attractive and varied forms of perennial salvias have something to offer every style of garden.

Growing

Most salvia plants prefer **full sun** but some tolerate light shade. The soil should be **moist**, **well drained** and of **average to rich fertility** with lots of **organic matter**.

Tips

Salvias look good grouped in beds and borders and in containers. The flowers are long lasting and make good cut flowers for arrangements.

To keep the plants producing flowers, water often and fertilize monthly.

There are over 900 species of Salvia ranging from perennials to annuals.

Features: red, blue, purple, burgundy, pink, orange, salmon, yellow, cream, white, bicolored summer through fall flowers; attractive foliage **Height:** 8"–4' **Spread:** 8"–4' **Hardiness:** zones 7–9

Recommended

There is a vast array of perennial salvias to choose from. The following are only a few of the best, but the selection is endless.

S. azurea (azure sage) is a 3' tall Southeast native sage with sky blue flowers that will stand up to both the heat and humidity.

S. '**Cherry Queen**' and *S.* '**Maraschino**' are reliable, red-flowering hybrids, and *S.* '**Indigo Spires**' produces bluish violet flower spikes.

Phlox

Phlox

P. paniculata 'Miss Pepper' (above)
P. paniculata cultivar (below)

Phlox comes in many shapes and sizes from low creepers to bushy border plants with flowering periods falling anywhere between early spring and mid-fall.

Growing

P. maculata and *P. paniculata* prefer **full sun**; *P. stolonifera* and *P. divaricata* prefer **light to partial shade** but tolerate heavy shade, and *P. subulata* prefers **full sun to partial shade**. All like **fertile, humus-rich, moist, well-drained** soil.
Divide in fall or spring.

Tips

Low-growing species are useful in rock gardens or at the front of borders. Taller phloxes may be used in the middle of borders and are particularly effective if planted in groups.

Recommended

P. divaricata (woodland phlox) produces slender stems covered in hairy, narrow leaves. It bears pale blue, white to pinkish white, open clusters of flowers. Cultivars are available in varying shades of pink, purple, blue or white. *P. maculata* (early phlox, garden phlox, wild sweet william) forms an upright clump of hairy stems and narrow leaves that are sometimes spotted with red. Pink, purple or white flowers are borne in conical clusters. *P. paniculata* (garden phlox, summer phlox) is an upright plant. The many cultivars vary in size and flower color. Look for mildew-resistant selections.

P. stolonifera (creeping phlox) is a low, spreading plant that bears flowers in several shades of purple to white. *P. subulata* (moss phlox, thrift) is very low growing and bears flowers in various colors. The foliage is narrow and evergreen.

Features: white, blue, purple, orange, pink, red spring or summer flowers **Height:** 2"–4' **Spread:** 12–36" **Hardiness:** zones 2–8

Pinks

Dianthus

From tiny and delicate to large and robust, this genus contains a wide variety of plants, many with spice-scented flowers.

Growing

Pinks prefer **full sun** but tolerate some light shade. A **well-drained, neutral or alkaline** soil is required. An important factor in the successful cultivation of pinks is drainage—they hate to stand in water. Rocky outcroppings are the native habitat of many species.

Tips

Pinks are excellent for rock gardens and rock walls, and for edging flower borders and walkways. They can be used in cutting gardens and even as groundcovers. To prolong blooming, deadhead as the flowers fade, but leave a few in place to go to seed.

Recommended

D. **x *allwoodii*** (allwood pinks) is a hybrid that forms a compact mound and bears flowers in a wide range of colors. Many cultivars are available.

D. deltoides (maiden pink) forms a mat of dark green foliage and flowers in white, deep pink or red, often with darker eyes.

D. deltoides (above)
D. gratianopolitanus 'Bath's Pink' (below)

D. gratianopolitanus (cheddar pink) is long-lived and forms a very dense mat of evergreen, silver gray foliage with sweet-scented flowers, mostly in shades of pink. **'Bath's Pink'** is a popular cultivar.

D. plumarius (cottage pink) is noteworthy for its role in the development of many popular cultivars known collectively as garden pinks. The flowers can be single, semi-double or fully double and are available in many colors.

Features: sometimes-fragrant spring or summer flowers in shades of pink, red, white, purple; attractive foliage **Height:** 2–18" **Spread:** 6–24" **Hardiness:** zones 3–9

Red-Hot Poker

Kniphofia

K. hybrid (above), *K. uvaria* cultivar (below)

This perennial is a great companion plant to many ornamental grasses and requires little to produce the fiery, spiky blooms.

Growing

These plants grow equally well in **full sun** or **partial shade**. The soil should be **fertile, humus rich, sandy** and **moist**. Ensure adequate water when the plant is blooming.

Large clumps may be divided in late spring, or in summer after flowering. The plants perform best when left undivided for several years.

Tips

Red-hot pokers make a bold, vertical statement in the middle or back of a border. They look best planted in groups made up of odd numbers. To encourage the plants to continue flowering for as long as possible, cut off the spent flowers where the flower stem emerges from the crown.

Recommended

K. hybrids include a vast number of selections but generally share the same narrow leaves and blooming period of *K. uvaria*. The fiery colors range from dusty coral and creamy white to tangerine orange and glowing yellow.

K. uvaria produces spikes of drooping, bright red to orange-red flower buds that open to yellow from late summer to early fall. Many cultivars are available in varied mature sizes and flower colors.

The flowers of red-hot poker are attractive to hummingbirds and butterflies. The blooms make long-lasting cut flowers and add bold accents to any floral arrangement.

Features: orange, yellow, chartreuse, red, white, coral flower spikes; **form Height:** 3–4' **Spread:** 18–24" **Hardiness:** zones 5–9

Spiderwort

Tradescantia

Spiderwort is a native plant with interesting, three-petaled flowers. It should repeat bloom if cut back after spring's first flowering, but requires little else for its success.

Growing

Spiderwort grows equally well in **full sun** or **partial shade** but appreciates some shade from the hot afternoon sun. The soil should be of **average fertility, humus rich** and **moist** but not soaked. If grown in too rich a soil with plentiful water, the plant can become weedy and fall open in the center.

Cutting the plants back after flowering has ceased will produce a fresh flush of foliage and possibly a second round of blooms late in the season. Divide in spring or fall every four or so years.

Tips

Spiderwort is attractive in a lightly shaded woodland or natural garden, but also looks good in beds and borders. Once established, spiderwort will grow almost anywhere.

Recommended

T. virginiana is a clump-forming perennial that grows 18" tall and wide. It bears strap-like foliage that arches gracefully from the stem. Three-petaled, blue, purple and sometimes

T. virginiana cultivar (above), T. virginiana (below)

white or pink flowers are produced in early summer, but each flower only lasts for one day; however, they continue to bloom for quite some time. A variety of selections are available with flowers in shades of blue, purple, pink or white, in varied forms and sizes.

Features: purple, blue, pink, white flowers in early summer; attractive foliage; easy to grow
Height: 16–24" **Spread:** 20–30"
Hardiness: zones 3–9

Tickseed

Coreopsis

C. verticillata 'Moonbeam' (above)
C. verticillata (below)

Tickseed produces flowers all summer and is easy to grow; it makes a fabulous addition to every garden.

Growing

Tickseed grows best in **full sun**. The soil should be of **average fertility, sandy, light** and **well drained**. Plants can develop crown rot in moist, cool locations with heavy soil. Too fertile a soil encourages floppy growth. Deadhead to keep plants blooming.

Tips

Tickseed is a versatile plant, useful in formal and informal borders and in meadow plantings and cottage gardens. It looks best when planted in groups.

Recommended

C. auriculata 'Nana' (mouse-eared coreopsis) is a low-growing species that bears yellow-orange flowers in late spring.

C. grandiflora (tickseed) is a native, clump-forming perennial that produces bright yellow flowers atop slender stems. Cultivar selections include semi-double and double flowers, differing bloom times and varied sizes.

C. lanceolata (lance coreopsis) is a native, clump-forming species with lance-shaped leaves and solitary, yellow flowers. Cultivars are available in dwarf forms and with double flowers.

C. rosea (rose coreopsis) has bright green foliage and pink flowers with yellow centers from summer to fall. **'Sweet Dreams'** has fine, needle-like foliage and bears large, white flowers with dark pinkish purple rings surrounding a central yellow eye.

C. verticillata (thread leaf coreopsis) is a mound-forming plant with attractive, finely divided foliage and bright yellow flowers. Available cultivars include **'Moonbeam,'** with pale yellow blooms and smaller, mature sizes.

Features: yellow, orange, white, pink summer flowers; attractive foliage
Height: 12–32" **Spread:** 12" to indefinite
Hardiness: zones 3–9

Toad Lily
Tricyrtis

These plants, with their peculiar spotted flowers, are sure to draw attention to their shaded garden corner each fall.

Growing

Toad lilies grow well in **partial, light** or **full shade**. The soil should be **fertile, humus rich, moist** and **well drained**.

Tips

These diminutive plants are well suited to plantings in woodland gardens and shaded borders. If you have a shaded rock garden, patio or pond, these plants make good additions to locations where you can get up close to take a good look at the often-spotted flowers.

Recommended

T. hirta forms a clump of light green leaves. It bears white to pale purple flowers spotted with dark purple in late summer and fall. Many wonderful cultivars are available with varied flower colors and patterns and foliar patterns.

T. hirta (above & below)

Toad lilies are great companion plants to coral bells (Heuchera), *hostas, impatiens, begonias and any fern selection.*

Also called: Japanese toad lily
Features: white, blue, purple flowers, with or without spots, in late summer and fall; attractive foliage **Height:** 24–36"
Spread: 12–24" **Hardiness:** zones 4–9

Verbena

Verbena

V. canadensis (above), *V. x hybrida* (below)

Verbena is an open, airy plant that will attract a plethora of butterflies to your garden.

Growing
Verbena grows best in **full sun**. The soil should be of average **fertility** and very **well drained**. Verbena is drought tolerant once established. Cut or pinch plants back by one-half in mid-season to encourage a lot of fall blooms.

Tips
Use verbena in the front or middle of beds and borders, and in containers to add height. Verbena self-seeds in abundance, but the seedlings are easy to keep under control. Because it

is such a wispy plant in flower, verbena looks best when mass planted.

Recommended
V. canadensis (rose verbena) bears rosy purple flowers atop a compact form. The species grows 1½' tall and 1½– 3' wide. Cultivars are available.

V. x hybrida (garden verbena) is a short-lived perennial that's also often grown as an annual. This hybrid is densely branched, producing grayish green foliage and compact clusters of white, pink, bright red, purple or blue flowers in solid colors or combinations. Other selections are available in colorful variations. **'Taylortown Red'** is a fine example of a red-blooming garden verbena.

Features: purple, red, white, pink, peach flowers in early to late summer; growth habit **Height:** 6–18" **Spread:** 18–36"
Hardiness: zones 6–9

Anise Tree
Illicium

*A*nise tree is an attractive, easy-to-grow, very pest-resistant shrub that grows and flowers exceptionally well in shaded conditions.

Growing
Anise tree grows well in **partial to full shade** in **moist, well-drained** soil with **a lot of organic matter** mixed in. It is tolerant of wet soils. Provide a location that is **sheltered** from the hot afternoon sun and that also provides shelter from winter winds.

Tips
Anise tree is very useful as a background plant in a shrub bed or mixed border. The dense foliage also makes anise trees useful as a screening plant. It is tolerant of pruning and can be used for hedges and espaliers. However, leave the shears in the shed and use hand pruners and proper pruning cuts. You can also train these plants as small, single-stemmed trees.

Recommended
I. anisatum (Japanese anise, star anise) is an upright, pyramidal to roundish shrub with shiny, medium to dark green foliage that has a pleasant licorice aroma when crushed or bruised. The creamy, yellowish green flowers bloom in spring and fade to white as they age. **'Pink Stars'** is an unusual pink-flowered form. Southern natives *I. floridanum* and *I. parviflorum* are also good, sturdy shrubs.

Also called: star anise **Features:** evergreen, broadly pyramidal shrub; flowers; foliage; fruit
Height: 6–10' **Spread:** 5–9'
Hardiness: zones: 7–9

I. anisatum (above & below)

Do not ingest any parts of I. anisatum *as all parts are highly toxic.*

Arborvitae
Thuja

T. plicata 'Zebrina'

Tips

The large varieties of arborvitae make excellent specimen trees; smaller cultivars can be used in foundation plantings and shrub borders and as formal or informal hedges.

Recommended

T. occidentalis (eastern arborvitae, white cedar) is a narrow, pyramidal tree with scale-like, evergreen needles. Dozens of cultivars are available. Two popular selections are **'Degroot's Spire,'** a slow-growing variety in an upright form, with deep green foliage and a mature size of 6' tall and 2' wide; and **'Golden Globe,'** a rounded, dwarf form with golden yellow foliage.

T. orientalis (oriental arborvitae) grows 25' tall and 15' wide but can grow larger. The species is rarely available but the cultivars and hybrids are highly sought after for their varied coloration, forms and overall diversity.

T. plicata (western arborvitae) is a narrowly pyramidal evergreen tree that grows quickly, resists deer browsing and maintains good foliage color all winter. Several cultivars are available, including dwarf and variegated varieties. **'Green Giant'** grows 3–5' annually, eventually reaching 30–50' heights and 10–20' spreads. (Zones 5–9)

Arborvitae are rot resistant, durable and long-lived evergreens, earning quiet admiration from gardeners everywhere.

Growing

Arborvitae prefer **partial shade** but tolerate light to partial sun. The soil should be of **average fertility, moist** and **well drained**. These plants enjoy humidity, and in the wild they are often found growing near marshy areas. Arborvitae will perform best in a location with some **shelter** from wind, especially in winter.

Features: small to large, evergreen shrub or tree; attractive foliage; bark; form
Height: 2–60' **Spread:** 2–25'
Hardiness: zones 2–8

Beautyberry

Callicarpa

*T*his florists' favorite adds pizzazz to your fall garden.

Growing

Beautyberry grows well in **full sun** or **light shade**. The soil should be of **average fertility** and **well drained**. Beautyberry is deciduous in the Southeast. Since it flowers and fruits on new wood, cut the entire shrub back in late winter for best results.

Tips

Beautyberries can be used in naturalistic gardens and in shrub and mixed borders where the uniquely colored fruit will add interest and contrast. The fruit-covered branches are often cut for fresh or dried arrangements, as the colorful fruit persists on cut and dried branches.

Features: bushy, deciduous shrub; arching stems that bear purple late-summer or fall fruit **Height:** 3–10' **Spread:** 3–6'
Hardiness: zones 5–10

Recommended

C. americana (American beautyberry) is a graceful, arching shrub that grows 8–10' tall and wide. It produces coarse leaves that are 6" long and provide pretty color in fall. This species has an open, loose growth habit. It bears lavender pink flowers in late spring, followed by violet clusters of fruit held well into winter.

C. japonica (Japanese beautyberry) is a large, open shrub with arching branches and decorative, purple fruit in fall. It can grow up to 10' tall and 4–6' wide. A white-fruited cultivar called **'Leucocarpa'** is available.

Beautyberry is known to fruit most prolifically in regions with long, hot summers. Planting beautyberry in groups will also ensure heavy fruit production.

Blue-Mist Shrub

Caryopteris

C. x *clandonensis* 'Dark Knight' (above)
C. x *clandonensis* (below)

Blue-mist shrub is cultivated for its aromatic stems, foliage and incredible blue flowers. A few cut stems in a vase will delicately scent a room.

Growing

Blue-mist shrub prefers **full sun,** but it tolerates light shade. It does best in soil of **average fertility** that is **light** and **well drained**. Wet and poorly drained soils can kill this plant. Blue-mist shrub is very drought tolerant once established.

Tips

Include blue-mist shrub in your shrub or mixed border. The bright blue, late-season flowers are welcome when many other plants are past their flowering best.

Recommended

C. x *clandonensis* (blue mist) forms a dense mound up to 4' tall and 3–5' in spread. It bears clusters of blue, purple or pink flowers in late summer and early fall. **'Arthur J. Simmonds'** has bright blue flowers and grayish green foliage with silvery undersides. **'Longwood Blue'** also has deep blue flowers complemented by silvery foliage, while **'Pink Chablis'** is a new cultivar with loads of soft pink flowers. **'Worchester Gold'** produces yellowish foliage and contrasting bluish purple flowers.

Features: rounded, spreading, deciduous shrub; attractive, fragrant foliage; twigs; summer flowers in shades of blue, purple, pink **Height:** 2–4' **Spread:** 2–5'
Hardiness: zones 5–9

Boxwood

Buxus

Boxwood's dense growth and small leaves form an even, green surface, which, along with its slow rate of growth, make it popular for creating low hedges and topiaries.

Growing

Boxwoods prefer **partial shade** but adapt to full sun if kept well watered. The soil should be **fertile** and **well drained**. Once established, boxwoods are drought tolerant. Try not to disturb the soil around established boxwoods because the roots are easily damaged.

Tips

Boxwoods make excellent background plants in a mixed border. Dwarf cultivars can be trimmed into small hedges for edging garden beds or walkways. An interesting topiary piece creates a formal or whimsical focal point in any garden. Larger species and cultivars are often used to form dense, evergreen hedges.

Recommended

B. microphylla var. *koreana* (Korean boxwood) grows about 4' tall, with an equal spread. The bright green foliage may turn bronze, brown or yellow in winter. It is hardy to zone 4. Cultivars are available.

B. sempervirens (common boxwood) can grow up to 20' tall, with an equal spread if it is not pruned. Cultivars are available in varied sizes and forms.

B. sempervirens (above), B. sempervirens x B. microphylla var. koreana culitvar (below)

'**Suffruticosa**' (edging boxwood) is a compact, slow-growing cultivar that's often used as hedging.

Some of the best boxwood selections are cultivars developed from crosses between the two listed species. These hybrids possess a high level of pest resistance, vigor and attractive winter color common to boxwood. CHICAGOLAND GREEN, '**Green Velvet**' and '**Green Mountain**' are all good selections.

Features: dense, rounded, evergreen shrub; attractive foliage **Height:** 2–20'
Spread: 2–20' **Hardiness:** zones 4–8

Camellia

Camellia

C. japonica 'Flame' (above), C. japonica cultivar (below)

Tips

Camellias are evergreen plants suitable for mixed beds, borders and woodland gardens, as specimens or as container plants. The soil should be 50% organic matter and 50% potting mix for container plantings .

Recommended

There are almost 300 species of camellias and thousands of cultivars. A few of the favorites include *C. japonica* (Japanese camellia), a large shrub or small tree that varies in growth rate, habit and size. It grows 6–12' tall and wide but larger specimens exist. Cultivars include **'White By The Gate,'** with large, double, white flowers. *C. olifera* (tea-oil camellia) is a large shrub or small tree with dark, glossy foliage and small, fragrant, white, fall flowers. *C. sasanqua* (sasanqua camellia) produces flowers smaller than *C. japonica*. It includes upright, tree-like, shrubby and spreading forms and can grow 6–15' tall. Cultivars include **'Jean May,'** bearing large pink flowers, **'Sparkling Burgundy'** with red-wine colored flowers and **'Yuletide'** with yellow-centered, single, red flowers. *C. sinensis* (tea plant) is a dense, rounded shrub that grows 15' tall and wide, with white, early-fall flowers. Pink-flowered cultivars are available.

Camellias tolerate salt and pollution, making them excellent choices for coastal and urban plantings.

Growing

Camellias prefer to grow in **light to partial shade** and in **well-drained, acidic to neutral** soil high in **organic matter**. *C. japonica* prefers an acidic soil. Protect camellias from strong, hot sun and drying winds. They may also suffer damage if temperatures drop below 15° F.

Features: upright to spreading shrub or small tree; colorful flowers; foliage **Height:** 18"–20', sometimes to 50' **Spread:** 3–12'
Hardiness: zones 7–9

Carolina Silverbell
Halesia

H. tetraptera (left & right)

$\mathcal{N}$ative to the Carolinas, this lovely specimen tree is a must-have for gardeners throughout the state who desire a prolific spring bloomer with so much to offer.

Growing
Carolina silverbell prefers **partial shade** but tolerates full sun. The soil should be **rich, moist** and very **well drained**. Amend the soil with organic matter. Mulching is imperative to prevent the soil from drying out. Prune as necessary but train a multi-stemmed specimen into a single-stemmed tree unless you want it to grow into a large shrub form. Prune only after flowering.

Tips
Carolina silverbell is commonly known as an understory tree, meaning it will grow quite happily under the canopy of larger trees. It is ideal for that moist location where few other trees will grow. This spring bloomer is the perfect specimen for the front yard. It will not overpower the front of the house, and dappled sunlight will travel through the branches providing light shade to plants below.

Recommended
H. tetraptera is a small to medium-sized tree that produces white, bell-shaped, pendent flowers along each branch in early spring. It displays an open form. Yellowish green fruit follows after the flowers, adding further interest in fall. Cultivars are available, including a pink-flowering selection called **'Rosea.'**

Features: open, low-branched, rounded, small to medium tree or shrub; white pendent flowers; form; attractive fruit **Height:** 30–40' **Spread:** 20–35' **Hardiness:** zones 5–8

Cedar
Cedrus

C. deodara (above), C. atlantica 'Glauca' (below)

Growing
Cedars grow well in **full sun** or **partial shade**. The soil can be of any type as long as it is **well drained**. A **moist, loamy** soil of **average to high fertility** is preferable.

Tips
Cedars are very large trees, best suited to large properties and parks.

Recommended
C. atlantica (atlas cedar, blue atlas cedar) is a large, wide-spreading, pyramidal tree with branches that sweep the ground. Smaller cultivars are available. **'Glauca Pendula'** is an interesting cultivar with trailing branches.

C. deodara (deodar cedar) is the largest and fastest growing cedar, but it is not reliably cold hardy in the mountains. It can grow to 100'. Cultivars more reasonable in size are often more tolerant of winter cold.

A mature cedar tree, with its towering form and elegant, layered, sweeping branches, is truly a magnificent sight to behold. Do not confuse the 'true cedars' (*Cedrus*) with the *Juniperus virginiana*, which we commonly refer to as 'cedar.'

C. libani (cedar of Lebanon) is often too big for the home garden, but it has cultivars that suit space-restricted settings.

A portrait of C. libani *graces the national flag of Lebanon.*

Features: large, upright, spreading or pendulous evergreen tree; foliage; cones; bark **Height:** 3–130' **Spread:** 15–40' **Hardiness:** zones 5–8

Crapemyrtle

Lagerstroemia

Crapemyrtles offer a unique element to just about any setting and require little care for stunning results.

Growing

Crapemyrtle performs best in **full sun** but tolerates light shade. It likes **well-drained, neutral to slightly acidic** soil. Hot winds may scorch the leaf margins. Ensure regular watering when young. Once established, crapemyrtle is quite drought tolerant but does best with an occasional deep watering. Do not water from overhead. Lightly prune and fertilize with organic fertilizer in late winter before new growth emerges.

Tips

Crapemyrtles make excellent specimens. *L. indica* can be used for street trees and in lawns. The shrubs can be used for hedging, screening, shrub borders and in mass plantings. Take care when underplanting around crapemyrtle—the roots are quite competitive. Long, cool fall seasons yield the best leaf color. Prune suckers as they appear and remove any newly emerging seedlings.

Recommended

L. fauriei (Japanese crapemyrtle) is a medium-sized tree with outward-arching branches in an erect form. It bears lush foliage, attractive bark and clusters of small, white flowers. **'Fantasy'** bears white flowers.

L. indica cultivar (above & below)

L. indica is a multi-stemmed, small tree. It bears showy clusters of ruffled, crepe-like flowers in white and shades of red, pink or purple in summer. The foliage begins as bronze-tinged light green, aging to dark glossy green in summer and turning yellow, orange or red in fall. The bark exfoliates to reveal the pinkish tan inner bark. Both standard and dwarf varieties are available, including **'Natchez,'** bearing white flowers and **'Tuskegee'** that bears deep pink red flowers.

Features: upright, deciduous tree or shrub, many-stemmed; flower clusters in shades of white, pink, red, purple, coral; exfoliating bark; fall color **Height:** 8–30' **Spread:** 6–16' **Hardiness:** zones 7–9

Cryptomeria
Cryptomeria

C. japonica 'Benjamin Franklin' (above)
C. japonica 'Radicans' (below)

What would a southern garden be without the graceful addition of a tall, evergreen specimen such as cryptomeria? With so much to offer year round, cryptomeria is a must-have tree for gardens throughout the state.

Growing

Cryptomeria prefers **full sun to light shade**. The soil should be **fertile, well drained, rich** and **deep**. Cryptomeria should be planted higher in the ground in heavily clay-based soils. Mulch well to prevent drying out during periods of drought.

Tips

Tall conifers are often used as specimens in residential landscapes and gardens. They're also planted for screening purposes.

Recommended

C. japonica is a vigorous-growing tree with a pyramidal habit and slightly pendulous branches. The needles are bright green to bluish green throughout the growing season but turn a brown-purple hue as the days grow cooler. An attractive, thin, reddish brown bark peels off the trunk and branches. **'Benjamin Franklin'** produces foliage that remains green year round, regardless of the temperatures, and is highly tolerant to wind and salt. It will grow into a tall tree form. **'Black Dragon'** bears light green foliage that darkens to almost black in fall. It grows more slowly, reaching only 5' tall and 7' wide over a 10-year period. **'Elegans'** is grayish green in color but turns a coppery red in winter. It can grow quite tall and wide. **'Yoshino'** is similar to the species, with a potential height of 30–40'.

Features: conical, columnar, coniferous tree or shrub; large; evergreen foliage; winter color; form **Height:** 1–100'
Spread: 1–30' **Hardiness:** zones 6–8

Dawn Redwood

Metasequoia

Dawn redwood is a refined, pyramidal tree with attractive, deeply furrowed, cinnamon red, flaking bark. Don't worry when this ancient tree drops its needles—it's deciduous.

Growing

Dawn redwood grows well in **full sun** or **light shade**. The soil should be **humus rich,** slightly **acidic, moist** and **well drained**. It tolerates wet or dry soils, but the growth rate is reduced in dry conditions. This tree likes humidity. Provide mulch and water regularly until it is established.

Tips

Dawn redwoods need plenty of room to grow. Large gardens and parks can best accommodate them.

The lower branches must be left in place in order for the trunk to develop its characteristic buttress. Buttressed trunks are flared and grooved, and the branches appear to be growing from deep inside the grooves.

M. *glyptostroboides* 'Ogon' (above)
M. *glyptostroboides* (below)

Recommended

M. glyptostroboides has a pyramidal, sometimes spire-like form. The needles turn gold or orange in fall before dropping. The cultivars are narrower than the species. **'Ogon'** has chartreuse foliage during the summer.

This tree is often called a 'living fossil' because it was discovered in fossil form before it was found growing in China in the 1940s.

Features: narrow, conical, deciduous conifer; foliage; bark; cones; buttressed trunk **Height:** 70–125' **Spread:** 15–25' **Hardiness:** zones 5–8

Dogwood
Cornus

C. kousa (above), C. kousa var. chinensis (below)

W hether your garden is dry, sunny or shaded, there is a dogwood for almost every condition.

Growing

Dogwoods grow well in **full sun, light shade** or **partial shade**, with a slight preference for light shade. The soil should be of **average to high fertility, high in organic matter, neutral or slightly acidic** and **well drained**.

Tips

Dogwoods can be included in a shrub or mixed border. The tree species make wonderful specimen plants and are small enough to include in most gardens. Use them along the edge of a woodland, alongside a house or near a pond, water feature or patio.

Recommended

C. florida (flowering dogwood) has slightly twisted or curled foliage that turns red and purple in fall. Green, yellow-tipped flowers are surrounded by white to pink bracts in spring, followed by red fruit. Cultivars are available with white, pink or red bracts. *C. kousa* (Kousa dogwood) has white-bracted flowers, followed by red fruit. The foliage turns red and purple in fall. **Var.** *chinensis* (Chinese dogwood) has larger flowers. **'Milky Way'** and **'Wolf Eyes'** bear pure white bracts. *C. mas* (Cornelian cherry) is a small shrub or tree with early-spring clusters of pale yellow blossoms on bare branches, followed by scarlet berries. **'Spring Glow'** bears yellow flowers and leathery, dark green leaves.

Features: deciduous or evergreen, large shrub or small tree; white, pink, ruby, yellow early-spring to early-summer flowers; fall foliage and fruit; stem color **Height:** 5–30' **Spread:** 5–30' **Hardiness:** zones 5–9

False Cypress
Chamaecyparis

C. pisifera 'Mops'

False cypresses offer color, size, shape and growth habits not available in most other evergreens.

Growing

False cypress prefers **full sun to partial shade**. The soil should be **fertile, moist, neutral to acidic** and **well drained**. Alkaline soils are tolerated. In shaded areas, growth may be sparse or thin.

Tips

Tree varieties are used as specimen plants and for hedging. The dwarf and slow-growing cultivars are used in borders, rock gardens and as bonsai. Shrubs can be grown near the house or as evergreen specimens in large containers.

Features: narrow, pyramidal, evergreen tree or shrub; attractive foliage; cones
Height: 2–70' **Spread:** 2–20'
Hardiness: zones 4–8

Recommended

There are several available species and cultivars of false cypress. The scaly foliage can be drooping or strand-like in form, have fan-like or feathery sprays and be dark green, bright green or yellow. Plant forms vary from mounding or rounded to tall and pyramidal or narrow with pendulous branches.

C. obtusa (Hinoki cypress) is a broad conical tree with dark green foliage and a mature size of up to 70'. Cultivars in smaller forms include **'Nana Gracilis'** that grows 6' tall in a pyramidal form. *C. pisifera* (Sawara or Japanese cypress) has an open habit and flattened sprays of bright green foliage. It grows up to 70' tall and 15' wide. Cultivars include **'Filifera'** (threadleaf cypress), bearing slender branches and dark green foliage, and **'Filifera Aurea,'** bearing golden yellow leaves at a 15–20' height. Check with your local garden center to see what is available.

Fatsia
Fatsia

F. japonica (above & below)

On a decorative container or mixed flowerbed, fatsia adds a tropical flair to just about any garden setting.

Growing
Fatsia requires **partial to full shade**. The soil should be **moist** but **well drained** and **fertile** in a location **sheltered** from cold, drying winds. Fatsia will sucker freely and it's not necessary to remove the shoot, but unwanted branches can be removed with a sharp spade. Cut back spindly plants in early spring. Self-sowing may occur if fruit is produced.

Tips
Fatsia produces a bold tropical form that is well suited to larger areas where an architectural element is required. It tolerates coastal conditions and thrives in sheltered shrub borders and patios.

Recommended
F. japonica (fatsia, Japanese fatsia, Japanese aralia) is a spreading, rounded and suckering evergreen shrub. It produces thick stems that support deeply lobed, large leaves that resemble hands with outstretched fingers. Each leaf can grow 6–16" long from base to tip. Creamy white flowers are produced in fall through winter, followed by shiny black berries. Many cultivars are available with variegated foliage and varied sizes.

Removing the berries will encourage the leaves to grow larger.

Features: spreading, rounded, evergreen shrub; large, ornate foliage and form; creamy white flowers; berries **Height:** 5–8' **Spread:** 5–8' **Hardiness:** zones 7–10

Flowering Quince

Chaenomeles

Beautiful in and out of flower, these plants create an attractive display as a specimen or when trained to grow up or along a brick wall.

Growing

Flowering quince grows well in **full sun**. It tolerates partial shade but produces fewer flowers. The soil should be of **average fertility, moist, slightly acidic** and **well drained**. These shrubs are tolerant of pollution and urban conditions.

Tips

Flowering quinces can be included in shrub and mixed borders. They are very attractive when grown against a wall, and their spiny habit makes them useful for barriers. Use these plants along the edge of a woodland or in a naturalistic garden. The dark stems stand out well in winter.

Recommended

C. speciosa (common flowering quince) is a large, tangled, spreading shrub. It grows 6–10' tall and spreads 6–15'. Red, white, pink or coral flowers are borne in late winter, followed by fragrant, greenish yellow fruit. Many cultivars are available, including the popular **'Toyo-Nishiki'** that produces red, pink or white flowers all on the

C. speciosa 'Texas Scarlet' (above & below)

same plant. **'Cameo'** is a low, compact selection with double, apricot-pink blooms. **'Jet Trail'** is also a low grower with pure white blossoms, while **'Texas Scarlet'** produces bright red flowers. This selection is also known for its fruit.

One of the loveliest of the later winter shrubs, quince adds drama and color on even the coldest days.

Features: spreading, deciduous shrub with spiny branches; red, pink, white, orange spring flowers; fragrant fruit **Height:** 2–10' **Spread:** 2–15' **Hardiness:** zones 5–8

Forsythia
Forsythia

F. x intermedia (above & below)

Growing

Forsythias grow best in **full sun**, but some selections tolerate or prefer **light or partial shade**. The soil should be of **average fertility, moist** and **well drained**. These plants are more cold hardy than their flower buds. Forsythias may flower in a colder-than-recommended hardiness zone if placed in a sheltered spot.

Tips

Forsythia shrubs are gorgeous while in flower. New selections with decorative foliage are being introduced to the market each year. Include forsythias in a shrub or mixed border where other flowering plants will provide interest once the forsythias' early-season glory has passed.

M ost gardeners remember forsythia as large, gangly shrubs that are prolific bloomers in early spring and quickly turn into large green blobs afterward; however, the introduction of new selections with more decorative foliage has made them much more appealing.

Forsythias can be used as hedging plants, but they look most attractive and flower best when grown informally.

Recommended

F. x *intermedia* is a large shrub with upright stems that arch as they mature. It grows 5–10' tall and spreads 5–12'. Bright yellow flowers emerge in early to mid-spring, before the leaves. Many cultivars are available. A few of the better selections include a dwarf selection called 'GOLD TIDE' and two new selections called '**Kumson**' and '**Fiesta.**'

Features: spreading, deciduous shrub with upright or arching branches; attractive, early to mid-spring yellow flowers **Height:** 2–10' **Spread:** 3–15' **Hardiness:** zones 5–8

Fothergilla
Fothergilla

Flowers that resemble bottle-brushes, fragrance, fall color and interesting, soft tan to brownish stems give fothergillas year-round appeal.

Growing

Fothergilla grows equally well in **full sun** or **partial shade**, but it bears the most flowers and has the best fall color in full sun. The soil should be of **average fertility, acidic, humus rich, moist** and **well drained**.

Tips

Fothergilla is attractive and useful in shrub or mixed borders, in woodland gardens and when combined with evergreen groundcover.

Recommended

F. gardenii (dwarf fothergilla) is a bushy, native shrub that bears fragrant, white flowers. The foliage turns yellow, orange and red in fall. It grows 2–3' tall and wide but can grow taller. Cultivars are available, including **'Blue Mist,'** which produces bluish foliage throughout the growing season.

F. major (large fothergilla) is very close in appearance to *F. gardenii* but is much larger in size. This native species grows 6–10' tall and wide but has been known to grow larger. **'Blue Shadow'** is an exceptional new cultivar with attractive, true blue foliage. **'Mt. Airy'** produces large flowers and fiery fall color. It grows 5–6' tall and wide.

F. major (above & below)

The bottlebrush-shaped flowers of fothergilla have a delicate, honey scent. The shrubs are generally problem free and make wonderful companions to azaleas, rhododendrons and other acid-loving, woodland plants.

Features: dense, rounded or bushy, deciduous shrub; fragrant, white spring flowers; fall foliage **Height:** 2–10' **Spread:** 2–10' **Hardiness:** zones 4–9

Fragrant Wintersweet
Chimonanthus

C. praecox (above & below)

Tips

This small group of large shrubs is cultivated and grown for its unique, golden, waxy and incredibly fragrant flowers. The flowers emerge earlier than the leaves in December through January. Certainly for winter interest, fragrant wintersweet is sure to attract some attention and, if nothing else, will emit the most lovely fragrance throughout your yard. This shrub can be pruned and trained into a small tree form. It can be best enjoyed within shrub borders along pathways and patios, where the fragrance can be appreciated.

The amazing fragrance produced by the flowers during winter is sure to distract you from its unassuming form and plain appearance.

Growing

Fragrant wintersweet thrives in **full sun** but tolerates partial sun. Locations with **fertile, well-drained** soil are best. Prune out old branches after flowering. A sheltered or protected location is often best to prevent possible bud damage.

Recommended

C. praecox is an upright, deciduous shrub with glossy, green leaves that follow pendent, pale yellow flowers with touches of brown and purple. Cultivars are available with a deeper yellow flower color, including **'Grandiflorus,'** which produces flowers that are larger but less fragrant than the species. **'Luteus'** bears bright yellow flowers, and **'Parviflorus'** has pale yellow flowers.

Chimonanthus is native to parts of China, and it was introduced into commerce in 1766.

Features: broadly upright, deciduous, multi-stemmed shrub; fragrant winter flowers; form
Height: 10–15' **Spread:** 8–12'
Hardiness: zones 7–9

Fringe Tree
Chionanthus

$\mathcal{F}$ ringe trees adapt to a wide range of growing conditions. They are cold hardy and are densely covered in silky, white, honey-scented flowers that shimmer in the wind over a long period in spring.

Growing

Fringe trees prefer **full sun**. They do best in soil that is **fertile, acidic, moist** and **well drained** but adapt to most soil conditions. In the wild they are often found growing alongside stream banks.

Tips

Fringe trees work well as specimen plants, as part of a border or beside a water feature. These plants begin flowering at a very early age.

Recommended

C. retusus (Chinese fringe tree) is a rounded, spreading shrub or small tree with deeply furrowed, peeling bark and erect, fragrant, white flower clusters. Most of the selections available are heavily flowering males. The classic deep blue fruits appear only on female plants.

C. virginicus (white fringe tree, grancy graybeard) is a spreading, small native tree or large shrub that bears drooping, fragrant, white flowers and dark blue fruit that wild birds enjoy eating.

C. virginicus (above & below)

The delicate flowers may be followed by small, dark fruit if both male and female plants are present. They are separate plants and the male specimens have larger flowers.

Features: rounded or spreading, deciduous, large shrub or small tree; fragrant, white early-summer flowers; bark **Height:** 10–25'
Spread: 10–25' **Hardiness:** zones 4–9

Gardenia

Gardenia

G. jasminoides (above & below)

Salty water can burn the foliage. Leach excess salt from the soil on a regular basis. Never use water that has been run through a water softener.

Gardenia has shallow roots that do not compete well if planted in a crowded situation. Avoid cultivating around the plant, use organic mulch instead.

Tips
Gardenias grow very well in containers and raised beds. They also make unusual hedges, espaliers and specimen plants.

Recommended
G. jasminoides (*G. augusta*) is an evergreen shrub that bears fragrant, cream to white flowers from summer to fall. Cultivars are available in varying plant and leaf sizes, with single or double flowers. Cold hardiness may be a factor in zone 7. In the western half of our state, ensure you select plants that can handle the colder conditions. **'Chuck Hayes'** grows 4' tall, bearing double flowers with a prolific rebloom in fall. **'Klein's Hardy'** is very cold tolerant and produces single flowers in summer. **'Radicans'** is a low-growing variety, growing 2' tall and 4' wide.

No southern garden should be without gardenia's intoxicating aroma.

Growing
Gardenia grows well in **full sun to light shade** in **well-drained, slightly acidic** soil. Plant in a location that provides **shelter** from cold winter winds. Wait until you see new growth in the spring to trim off any winterburn. If cold kills the plants to the ground, they should regenerate from the roots.

Features: upright to rounded evergreen tree or shrub; intensely fragrant flowers; foliage **Height:** 4–6' **Spread:** 4–8'
Hardiness: zones 8–11

Ginkgo
Ginkgo

Be patient with ginkgo—its gawky, irregularly angular youth will eventually pass to reveal a spectacular mature specimen tree.

Growing

Ginkgo prefers **full sun**. The soil should be **fertile, sandy** and **well drained**, but this tree adapts to most conditions. It is also tolerant of urban conditions, pollution and cold weather.

Tips

Although its growth is very slow, ginkgo eventually becomes a large tree that is best suited as a specimen tree in parks and large gardens. It can be used as a street tree. If you buy an unnamed plant, be sure it has been propagated from cuttings. Seed-grown trees may prove to be female, and the odiferous fruit is not something you want dropping onto your lawn, driveway or sidewalk.

Recommended

G. biloba is variable in habit. The unique fan-shaped leaves can turn an attractive shade of yellow in fall. Several cultivars are available, including **'Autumn Gold,'** a tall specimen with a broad and spreading habit; **'Fastigiata,'** an upright columnar form, and the dwarf **'Jade Butterfly**. **'Saratoga'** is a small specimen with an unusually dense crown made up of decorative, split leaves.

G. biloba (above & below)

Ginko is renowned for its many medicinal properties.

Features: conical in youth, variable with age; deciduous tree; summer and fall foliage; fruit; bark **Height:** 30–80' **Spread:** 10–30' **Hardiness:** zones 3–8

Glossy Abelia
Abelia

A. x grandiflora (above & below)

This vigorous shrub is covered with pink buds in spring that open to white blooms, creating a wonderful garden display that you and the butterflies will both enjoy.

Growing

Glossy abelia grows well in **full sun** or **partial shade**. The soil should be **fertile, relatively moist** and **well drained**. Some pruning is required right after flowering to keep it full and tidy.

Tips

Glossy abelia makes a lovely addition to a shrub or mixed border. Because it is a relatively large shrub, it is best suited to the back of the border.

Recommended

A. x *grandiflora* is a rounded, evergreen or semi-evergreen shrub with arching branches covered in dark green, glossy foliage.

Funnel-shaped flowers are borne in mid-summer and continue to emerge until fall. The flowers are fragrant and white in color, but touched with a hint of pink. Cultivars are available with variegated foliage and other unique qualities, including **'Little Richard,'** a dwarf cultivar, 3' tall and wide, with a dense growth habit and white flowers. **'Sunrise'** was discovered at Taylor's Nursery in Raleigh, NC, and it produces golden and creamy white variegated foliage.

Features: rounded to upright semi-evergreen shrub, with glossy foliage that turns orange to red in fall; white spring flowers **Height:** 3–10' **Spread:** 3–6' **Hardiness:** zones 4–8

Golden Rain Tree

Koelreutaria

K. paniculata (above & below)

With its delicate clusters of yellow flowers and overall lacy appearance in summer, this lovely tree deserves wider use as a specimen or shade tree.

Growing

Golden rain tree grows best in **full sun**. The soil should be **average to fertile, moist** and **well drained**. This tree tolerates heat, drought, wind, and air pollution. It also adapts to most pH levels and is fast-growing.

Tips

Golden rain tree makes an excellent shade or specimen tree for small properties. Its ability to adapt to a wide range of soils makes it useful in many garden situations. The fruit is not messy and will not stain a patio or deck.

Features: rounded, spreading, deciduous tree; attractive foliage; fruit; yellow summer flowers **Height:** 30–40' **Spread:** 30–40' **Hardiness:** zones 5–8

Recommended

K. paniculata is an attractive, rounded, spreading tree. It bears long clusters of small, yellow flowers in summer, followed by red-tinged, green capsular fruit. The leaves are attractive and somewhat lacy in appearance. The foliage may turn bright yellow in fall. Cultivars are available, including **'Fastigiata,'** which grows 25' tall and only 3' wide, and **'Rose Lantern,'** a late bloomer that bears rose pink fruit capsules for up to six weeks.

This Asian species is one of the few trees with yellow flowers.

Holly

Ilex

I. cornuta 'Carissa'

ollies vary greatly in shape and size and are such delights when placed with full consideration for their needs.

Growing

These plants prefer **full sun** but tolerate partial shade. The soil should be of **average to rich fertility, humus rich** and **moist.** Hollies perform best in **acidic** soil with a pH of 6.5 or lower. Shelter hollies from winter wind to prevent the evergreen leaves from drying out. Apply a summer mulch to keep the roots cool and moist.

Tips

Hollies can shaped into hedges or can be used in groups, in woodland gardens and in shrub and mixed borders.

Recommended

There is an unending array of hollies. Consult your local garden center for their recommendations. *I. cornuta* (Chinese holly) is an evergreen shrub or small tree that is tolerant of excessive heat. *I. crenata* (Japanese holly) closely resembles boxwood. *I. glabra* is a moisture-loving evergreen that grows 10' tall. *I.* **hybrids** offer every form, size and special characteristic available. *I. latifolia* is often confused with southern magnolia, *M. grandifolia,* when young, but is one of largest hollies available. *I. opaca* (American holly) grows 40–50' tall but takes a lifetime to get there. *I. verticillata* (winterberry, winterberry holly) is a deciduous, native species grown for its explosion of red, orange or yellow fruit that persists into winter. *I. vomitoria* (Yaupon holly) is a small-leaved native often used as tall, dense hedging material and is tolerant of a coastal environment.

Features: erect or spreading, evergreen or deciduous shrub or tree; attractive, glossy, sometimes spiny, foliage; fruit **Height:** 3–50' **Spread:** 3–40' **Hardiness:** zones 3–9

Hydrangea
Hydrangea

Hydrangeas have many attractive qualities, including showy, often long-lasting flowers and glossy green leaves, some of which turn beautiful colors in fall.

Growing

Hydrangeas grow well in **full sun** or **partial shade** but some species tolerate full shade. Shade or partial shade reduces leaf and flower scorch in hotter gardens. The soil should be of **average to high fertility, humus rich, moist** and **well drained**. These plants perform best in cool, moist conditions.

Tips

Hydrangea shrubs come in many forms and have many uses in the landscape. They can be included in shrub or mixed borders, used as specimens or informal barriers and planted in groups or containers.

Recommended

H. arborescens (smooth hydrangea) is a rounded, native shrub. Cultivars such as **'Annabelle'** and WHITE DOME are more available than the species and bear large, rounded clusters of white flowers.

H. macrophylla (bigleaf hydrangea, garden hydrangea) is a large, rounded shrub with flowerheads of red, blue, pink or white. Cultivars can have either rounded, mophead or lacecap flowers.

H. quercifolia (above), *H. macrophylla* (below)

H. paniculata (panicle, P.G. hydrangea) is a spreading to upright, large shrub or small tree, bearing white flowers from late summer to early fall. Cultivars are available.

H. quercifolia (oakleaf hydrangea) is a native, mound-forming shrub with brown, exfoliating bark and leaves reminiscent of oak leaves that turn bright red in fall. Many cultivars are available with large flower clusters.

Features: deciduous, mounding or spreading shrub or tree; attractive flowers in shades of purple, pink, white, blue; foliage; bark
Height: 3–22' **Spread:** 3–15'
Hardiness: zones 4–9

Indian Hawthorn

Rhaphiolepis

R. indica (above & below)

Indian hawthorn is the ideal shrub for hot, sunny locations when protected from drying winds. It will thrive where azaleas melt from the heat, offering a profusion of fragrant, pink or white flowers and lush evergreen foliage.

Growing

Indian hawthorn prefers a location in **full sun**, protected from cold, drying winds. It tolerates partial shade. The soil should be very **well drained, moderately fertile** and **slightly alkaline**. Harsh winters can burn the foliage in the Piedmont when planted in exposed areas.

Tips

Flowering shrubs are always ideal for mixed borders, but this low-maintenance specimen is ideal for tiered landscapes to best display its graceful habit. With adequate mulching and irrigation during its first season, this shrub becomes drought and heat tolerant, making it popular with coastal gardeners for use in their seaside gardens.

Recommended

R. indica is a bushy evergreen shrub with a slight spreading habit. It produces dark green, leathery leaves with bronze undersides and white flower clusters with pink-tinged centers. Many cultivars are available. A few to watch for include **'Eleanor Tabor'**, a mounding, pink-flowering hawthorn; **'Olivia,'** which bears pure white flower clusters; and **'Pink Lady'** with pink flowers. All these selections are highly resistant to leaf spot.

Features: bushy, slightly spreading, evergreen shrub; abundance of white or pink flowers; evergreen foliage; heat tolerance **Height:** 4–5' **Spread:** 4–5' **Hardiness:** zones 7–10

Japanese Aucuba
Aucuba

This tough plant is tolerant of frost, pollution, deep shade, salty, windy coastal conditions and neglect. The foliage and berries are a dynamic addition to any garden.

Growing
Japanese aucuba grows well in **partial to full shade** in **moderately fertile, humus-rich, moist, well-drained** soil. Plants with variegated foliage show the best leaf color in partial shade. This plant adapts to most soil conditions as long as the soil is not waterlogged, and it tolerates urban pollution.

Tips
Japanese aucuba can be used in deeply shaded locations where no other plants will grow, such as under the canopy of larger trees. It can also be used as a specimen, in a large planter and as a hedge or screen.

Generally, both a male and female plant must be present for the females to set fruit. The fruits are not edible.

Recommended
A. japonica **'Nana'** is a compact plant with erect stems, a neatly rounded habit and glossy green leaves. It grows 3–4' tall and wide. Female plants develop red berries in fall. The fruit is highly visible as it is held above the foliage.

A. japonica cultivar (above & below)

Many cultivars of *A. japonica* are available, usually grown for their variegated foliage. The species is twice the size of 'Nana.' **'Picturata'** has a well-defined, dark yellow center on each leaf, and **'Variegata'** (gold dust plant) has dark green leaves spotted with yellow.

Also called: dwarf Japanese aucuba
Features: bushy, rounded, evergreen shrub; foliage; fruit; adaptability **Height:** 4–10'
Spread: 3–4' **Hardiness:** zones 7–10

Japanese Cleyera
Ternstroemia

T. gymnanthera (above)
T. gymnanthera 'Burnished Gold' (below)

This relative of the camellia is another ornamental shrub that thrives in shady spots, offering glistening, evergreen foliage and a tough constitution.

Growing

Japanese cleyera prefers **partial shade** in locations with **moist** but **well-drained, humus-rich, acidic** soil. Mulching and thorough watering in the first two years will prepare it for bouts of drought, once it is established.

Pruning may be necessary to remove wispy, leggy branches and maintain its symmetrical form. This is especially the case when grown in dense shade.

Tips

Japanese cleyera is often used as informal hedging, within a mixed shrub and perennial border or as a specimen or pondside plant.

Recommended

T. gymnanthera is a rounded, evergreen shrub with glossy, leathery leaves. The leaves emerge bronze but turn dark green over time. The leaves are also known to change from green to bronze in cold weather. Creamy yellow to white, inconspicuous, fragrant flowers are borne in spring, followed by yellow to red-orange berries. **'Burnished Gold'** produces new growth that is golden in color but fades to a bronzy green. **'Grewald'** (Copper Crown) is a burgundy-leaved cultivar, and **'Variegata'** has dark green leaves with a creamy white edge that turns pink as the days grow cooler in fall.

This pest-free shrub is a great companion and complement to azaleas and spring-flowering shrubs. It will also substitute for red tip photinia (Photinia x fraseri) *and Leyland cypress* (x Cupressocyparis leylandii).

Features: rounded, evergreen shrub; shiny, evergreen foliage; creamy yellow to white, inconspicuous flowers **Height:** 10'
Spread: 6' **Hardiness:** zones 7–9

Japanese Kerria

Kerria

The bright yellow, spring-blooming flowers, yellow fall foliage and distinctive, yellow-green to bright green arching stems make Japanese kerria an excellent addition to a garden.

Growing

Japanese kerria prefers **light, partial** or **full shade**. The soil should be of **average fertility** and **well drained**. Soil that is too fertile will produce a plant with few flowers. Prune after flowering. Cut the flowering shoots back to young side shoots or strong buds, or right to the ground. The entire plant can be cut back to the ground after flowering if it becomes overgrown and needs rejuvenating.

Tips

Try planting Japanese kerria in group plantings, woodland gardens and shrub or mixed borders. Sporadic flowers may appear in summer.

Recommended

K. japonica has single, yellow flowers. Cultivars are available with variegated foliage, double yellow flowers and white to light yellow flowers.

K. japonica 'Golden Guinea' (above)
K. japonica (below)

Japanese kerria's yellow-green to bright green stems add interest to a winter landscape.

Features: suckering, mounding, deciduous shrub; yellow, white, mid- to late-spring flowers
Height: 3–10' **Spread:** 4–10'
Hardiness: zones 4–8

Juniper
Juniperus

J. virginiana 'Blue Arrow' (above)
J. conferta 'Emerald Sea' (below)

There may be a juniper in every gardener's future with all the choices available, from low-creeping plants to upright, pyramidal forms.

Growing

Junipers prefer **full sun** but tolerate light shade. Ideally, the soil should be of **average fertility** and **well drained**, but these plants tolerate most conditions.

Tips

With the wide variety of junipers available, there are endless uses for them in the garden. They make prickly barriers and hedges and can be used in borders, as specimens or in groups. The larger species can be used to form windbreaks, while the low-growing species can be used in rock gardens and as groundcover.

Recommended

Junipers vary, not just from species to species, but often within a species. Cultivars are available for all species and may differ significantly from the species. *J. chinensis* (Chinese juniper) is a conical tree or spreading shrub. *J. communis* is a native, low-growing, spreading species. *J. conferta* and *J. horizontalis* (creeping juniper) are prostrate, creeping groundcovers. *J. davurica* and *J. procumbens* (Japanese garden juniper) are both wide-spreading, stiff-branched, low shrubs. *J. scopulorum* (Rocky Mountain juniper) can be upright, rounded, weeping or spreading. *J. squamata* (singleseed juniper) forms a prostrate or low, spreading shrub or a small, upright tree. *J. virginiana* (eastern redcedar) is a durable, upright or wide-spreading tree.

Juniper 'berries' are poisonous if eaten in large quantities.

Features: conical or columnar tree; rounded or spreading shrub; prostrate groundcover; evergreen **Height:** 4"–80' **Spread:** 1½–25' **Hardiness:** zones 3–9

Loropetalum
Loropetalum

L. chinense cultivar (above & below)

Loropetalum is an attractive, winter-flowering shrub that can be used almost anywhere an evergreen shrub is needed or wanted. And the reddish purple-leaved varieties are a knock-out!

Growing

Loropetalum grows best in **full sun** and almost as good in partial or light shade. The ideal soil is **acidic, moist** and **well drained** with **a lot of organic matter** mixed in, but loropetalum adapts to sandy or clay soils. In the northern half of the Carolinas it is best to plant loropetalum in a location sheltered from cold winter winds and to provide some protection when the temperature dips below 0° F.

Features: low-growing, spreading, evergreen shrub; winter flowers in various shades of pink or white; attractive foliage; low-maintenance
Height: 4–6' **Spread:** 4–6'
Hardiness: zones 5–9

Tips

Loropetalum can be used in a wide variety of shrub and mixed beds and borders. The evergreen foliage makes a nice background for other flowering plants.

Recommended

L. chinense is a fast-growing, irregular, rounded to upright shrub with glossy, dark green, evergreen foliage and fragrant, creamy white flowers. There are also a number of excellent reddish purple-leaved selections that have pink flowers, including the compact **'Ruby'** that grows 6' tall, **'Sizzling Pink'** and **'Zhuzhou Fuchsia'** with nearly black foliage.

Magnolia
Magnolia

M. *grandiflora* cultivar (above), M. x *soulangeana* (below)

Magnolias are beautiful, fragrant, versatile plants that also provide attractive winter structure.

Growing
Magnolias grow well in **full sun or partial shade**. The soil should be **fertile, humus rich, acidic, moist** and **well drained**. A summer mulch will help keep the roots cool and the soil moist.

Tips
Magnolias are used as specimen trees, and the smaller species can be used in borders.

Avoid planting magnolias where the morning sun will encourage the blooms to open too early in the season. Cold, wind and rain can damage the blossoms.

Recommended
Many species, hybrids and cultivars, in a range of sizes and with differing flowering times and colors are available. A few of the most common include *M. acuminata* (cucumber tree), which is one of the most stately, native, deciduous magnolias. It bears dark green leaves with downy undersides and cup-shaped, lightly scented, greenish yellow flowers, followed by green cucumber-shaped fruit that ripens to a deep red. *M. ashei* (ashe magnolia) and *M. macrophylla* (bigleaf magnolia) produce very large leaves and flowers. *M. grandiflora* (Southern magnolia) is the classic evergreen native tree form that can grow 80' tall. *M. x soulangeana* (saucer magnolia) is a rounded, spreading, deciduous shrub or tree with pink, purple or white flowers; and *M. stellata* (star magnolia), a compact, bushy or spreading, deciduous shrub or small tree with many-petaled, fragrant white flowers.

Features: upright to spreading, deciduous shrub or tree; white, pink, purple, yellow, cream, apricot flowers; fruit; foliage; bark
Height: 8–70' **Spread:** 5–30'
Hardiness: zones 4–8

Mahonia
Mahonia

Mahonia can be used by itself or, better yet, as a transition plant between a woodland garden and a more formal garden. The blue berries are edible and make a wonderful jelly.

Growing

Mahonia grows in **full sun to light shade**. The soil should be **well drained** and **neutral to slightly acidic**.

Tips

Use these shrubs in mixed or shrub borders and in woodland gardens. Low-growing specimens can be used as groundcovers.

Recommended

M. aquifolium (Oregon grape holly) is a suckering shrub that produces yellow flowers in spring, followed by clusters of purple or blue berries. The foliage turns a bronze-purple color in late fall and winter. Low-mounding cultivars are also available.

M. bealei (leatherleaf mahonia) produces strong, upright stems covered in leathery, blue-green foliage. Yellow flowers emerge in winter, only to be replaced 4–6 weeks later with clusters of bluish purple fruit.

M. japonica is an erect shrub, clothed in sharply toothed leaves and pale yellow, fragrant flowers, followed by purple-blue berries.

M. aquifolium (above & below)

M. repens (Creeping mahonia) is a low-growing shrub that spreads by suckers. The dull green leaves turn a bronze color in late fall and winter. Small clusters of lightly fragrant, yellow flowers are produced in mid- to late spring, followed by blue-black berries.

Features: upright, spreading, evergreen shrub; yellow, late-winter to early-spring flowers; summer fruit; late-fall and winter evergreen foliage **Height:** 1–10'
Spread: 3–10' **Hardiness:** zones 5–10

Maple
Acer

A. palmatum 'Sango Kaku' (above), A. japonicum (below)

M aples are attractive all year, with delicate flowers in spring, attractive foliage in summer, vibrant leaf color in fall and interesting bark and branch structures in winter.

Growing

Generally, maples do well in **full sun** or **light shade,** though this varies from species to species. The soil should be **fertile, moist, high in organic matter** and **well drained**.

Tips

Maples can be used as specimen trees, as large elements in shrub or mixed borders or as hedges. Some are useful as understory plants bordering wooded areas; others can be grown in containers on patios or terraces. Few Japanese gardens are without the attractive, smaller maples. Almost all maples can be used to create bonsai specimens.

Recommended

Maples are some of the most popular trees used as shade or street trees. Many are very large when fully mature, but there are also a few smaller species that are useful in smaller gardens, including *A. campestre* (hedge maple), *A. ginnala* (amur maple), *A. griseum* (paperbark maple), *A. japonicum* (full-moon maple), *A. palmatum* (Japanese maple) and *A. rubrum* (red maple). Check with your local nursery or garden center for availability.

Features: small, multi-stemmed, deciduous tree or large shrub; foliage; bark; winged fruit; fall color; form; flowers **Height:** 6–80' **Spread:** 6–70' **Hardiness:** zones 2–8

Mountain Laurel

Kalmia

*Y*ou'll stop cold to look at the large, colorful flower clusters produced by this underused shrub.

Growing

Mountain laurel prefers **light or partial shade**. The soil should be of **average to high fertility, moist, acidic** and **well drained**. Mountain laurel does not perform well in alkaline soil. A mulch of leaf mold or pine needles keeps the roots of this drought-sensitive plant from drying out.

Tips

Use mountain laurel in a shaded part of a shrub or mixed border, in a woodland garden or combine it with other acid- and shade-loving plants, such as rhododendrons.

The flowers and foliage of *Kalmia* are **poisonous** and should not be consumed.

Recommended

K. angustifolia (sheep laurel) is a mound-forming shrub, bearing dark evergreen foliage and pale to deep red, occasionally white, flowers. Cultivars are available in shades of pink, red or white. **'Rubra'** produces deep rosy red clusters of saucer-shaped flowers. This species performs best in the colder regions of the Carolinas.

K. latifolia 'Sarah' (above), *K. latifolia* 'Fresca' (below)

K. latifolia (mountain laurel) is a dense and bushy shrub with glossy, dark evergreen leaves. Large clusters of pale to deep pink, occasionally white, flowers emerge in late spring to mid-summer. The flower buds appear 'crimped' towards the tip and are darker in color compared to other species. Many cultivars are available, but **'Olympic Fire'** stands out. It bears wavy margined leaves and large, pink clusters of flowers emerging from red buds.

Features: mound-forming, bushy, evergreen shrub; large flower clusters in shades of white, pink, red, coral, bicolored, solid; form
Height: 3–10' **Spread:** 3–10'
Hardiness: zones 4–9

Oak

Quercus

Q. alba (above), Q. virginiana (below)

The oak's classic shape, outstanding fall color, hardiness and long life are some of its many assets. Plant it for its individual beauty and for posterity.

Growing

Oaks grow well in **full sun** or **partial shade**. The soil should be **fertile, moist** and **well drained**. These trees can be difficult to establish; transplant them only when they are young.

Tips

Oaks are large trees that are best as specimens or for groves in parks and large gardens. Do not disturb the ground around the base of an oak; it is very sensitive to changes in grade.

Recommended

There are many oaks to choose from. A few popular species are **Q. alba** (white oak), a rounded, spreading, native tree with peeling bark and purple-red fall color; **Q. coccinea** (scarlet oak), noted for having the most brilliant, red fall color of all the oaks; **Q. palustris** (pin oak), a vigorous, conical tree with pendent lower branches and deeply lobed leaves; and **Q. virginiana** (live oak), a massive, wide-spreading native tree that has reddish brown bark and leathery, small, dark evergreen leaves. This species is best grown in the warmest areas of zone 7–8. Some cultivars are available; check with your local nursery or garden center.

Features: large, rounded, spreading, deciduous tree; summer and fall foliage; bark; acorns **Height:** 35–120' **Spread:** 10–100' **Hardiness:** zones 3–9

Osmanthus
Osmanthus

Osmanthus, also commonly known as tea olives, is the perfect complement to the winter landscape, offering fragrant flowers and evergreen foliage.

Growing
Osmanthus prefers to grow in a location with **full to partial sun, sheltered** from the winter sun and wind. The soil should be **fertile, well drained** and **neutral to acidic.**

Tips
Most osmanthus selections grow to be large shrubs, which are ideal for tall privacy screens and hedging. Accepting of pruning, osmanthus can be trained as a small specimen tree for smaller yards and gardens and is perfect for naturalizing.

Recommended
O. x *fortunei* (Fortune's osmanthus) is a slow-growing, upright shrub with leathery, but glossy, holly-like foliage and tubular white flowers that emit a sweet scent in late fall. Cultivars are available with varied flower colors and forms. (Zones 7–8)

O. fragrans (fragrant tea olive) is a dense, compact shrub with an upright form. It bears leathery, toothed foliage with a glossy surface. Fragrant, white flowers are produced in late fall and sporadically return in spring, followed by blue-black fruit. Cultivars are available with yellow or orange blossoms. (Zones 9–10)

Features: slow-growing, upright, dense, compact, rounded shrub; shiny, ornate, evergreen foliage; form; white, orange, yellow, cream flowers **Height:** 8–20' **Spread:** 6–10' **Hardiness:** zones 7–10

O. heterophyllus cultivar (above), *O.* x *fortunei* (below)

O. heterophyllus (holly osmanthus, false holly) is a dense, rounded shrub at maturity, bearing sharply toothed, holly-like foliage. Tubular, fragrant, white flowers are produced in fall, followed by bluish black fruit. **'Goshiki'** bears yellow margined, mottled and pink-orange tinged leaves that mature to creamy yellow on dark green. (Zones 6–9)

Pieris

Pieris

P. japonica 'Mountain Fire' (above), P. japonica (below)

Need a shrub that doesn't lose its leaves or need pruning, blooms in late winter and rarely has pest problems? Pieris fits the bill and adds fragrance to the garden as a bonus.

Growing

Pieris grows equally well in **full sun** or **partial shade**. The soil should be of **average fertility, acidic, humus rich, moist** and **well drained**. Gardeners not in mild, coastal areas should ensure pieris has a **sheltered location** protected from the hot sun and drying winds.

Pieris' flower buds form in late summer the year before it flowers, so even unopened they provide an attractive show all winter long.

Tips

Pieris can be used in a shrub or mixed border, in a woodland garden or as a specimen. Try grouping it with rhododendrons and other acid-loving plants.

Recommended

P. japonica bears white flowers in long, pendulous clusters at the ends of its branches. Several dwarf cultivars are available, as are cultivars with bright red new foliage, variegated foliage and pink flowers. **'Mountain Fire,' 'Snowdrift'** and **'Temple Bells'** are fine examples for southern gardens.

Also called: lily-of-the-valley shrub
Features: compact, rounded, evergreen shrub; colorful new growth; late-winter to spring flowers **Height:** 3–12' **Spread:** 3–10'
Hardiness: zones 5–8

Plum Yew

Cephalotaxus

This yew-like shrub offers all of the visual qualities of a yew but has a higher tolerance to heat and is much less attractive to deer.

Growing

Plum yews prefer locations in **partial shade** but may tolerate full sun. The soil should be **moist, fertile** and **well drained**. Locations **sheltered** from wind are best.

Tips

This evergreen shrub is excellent for planting en masse for added impact and will thrive in foundation plantings. Plum yews are also tolerant of hard clipping, making them ideal for hedging material. They make fine specimens all on their own and mix well into borders and beds.

Recommended

C. harringtonia (plum yew, Japanese plum yew) is a coniferous evergreen shrub and occasionally a small tree. It bears sharply pointed, slightly curved, needle-like leaves. Cultivars are available in taller, upright, low-growing and spreading forms as well, including **'Duke Gardens,'** which grows only 3–4' tall and wide; **'Fastigiata,'** a more upright columnar form that grows 10' tall; and **'Korean Gold,'** which produces golden foliage.

C. harringtonia 'Fastigiata' (above)
C. harringtonia 'Duke Gardens' (below)

This particular species is native to parts of Korea and Japan. Other species hail from NE India, Burma, Vietnam, China and Taiwan.

Features: coniferous, upright, rounded to sprawly tree or shrub; evergreen foliage; form **Height:** 3–10' **Spread:** 3–10' **Hardiness:** zones 6–9

Poet's Laurel

Danae

D. racemosa (above & below)

Tips

Poet's laurel love of shade will help to determine where this beauty should be planted. Shrub borders are an ideal location if adequately protected from direct sun to prevent the leaves from become marked and faded. The tiny, white flowers emerge in spring, followed by orange-red berries in fall, which makes this shrub a great candidate for borders lacking a little spring color or persistent berry color throughout the winter months.

Recommended

D. racemosa (poet's laurel, Alexandrian laurel) is a small, dense, evergreen shrub with a graceful habit and arching stems. Each stem is clothed in leaf-like foliage, called cladophylls, which aren't really leaves at all but are modified, flattened stems that resemble leaves. Tiny, white flowers are produced in spring, followed by orange-red cherry-sized berries.

This pest-free, graceful shrub is deserving of wider use throughout the state. Shady borders crying out for a smaller, evergreen specimen have a fine option available in poet's laurel.

Growing

Poet's laurel prefers **partial to full shade, shielded from direct sun**. The soil should be **moist** but **well drained, fertile** and **humus rich**.

The genus Danae *is named for Danaë, the daughter of King Aerisius of Argos. The branches can be cut for winter bouquets and are known to last for long periods in a vase.*

Features: small, dense, graceful, arching evergreen shrub; lustrous foliage; persistent berries; white flowers **Height:** 2–4'
Spread: 2–4' **Hardiness:** zones 7b–9

Prunus

Prunus

Ornamental flowering selections from *Prunus* are so beautiful and uplifting after the gray days of winter that few gardeners can resist them.

Growing

Prunus prefers **full sun**. The soil should be of **average fertility, moist** and **well drained**. Shallow roots emerge from the lawn if the tree is not getting sufficient water.

Tips

Prunus are beautiful as specimen plants and many are small enough to be included in almost any garden. Smaller species and cultivars can be included in borders or grouped to form informal hedges or barriers.

Recommended

P. campanulata (Formosan cherry) is a very early-blooming species. 'Okame' is a bushy tree or shrub with orange-red fall foliage and carmine red blossoms. *P. caroliniana* (Carolina cherry laurel) is an upright, evergreen shrub with small, creamy white, late-winter or early-spring flowers. *P. glandulosa* (dwarf flowering almond) is a rounded, deciduous shrub, bearing white to pale pink flowers. *P. laurocerasus* (English cherry laurel) is a dense, bushy, evergreen shrub with fragrant, white

P. subhirtella 'Pendula Rosea' (above)

flowers. *P. mume* (Japanese flowering apricot) is a spreading, deciduous tree with fragrant, white or pink flowers. *P. serrulata* is a rounded tree with peeling, glossy copper bark, white spring flowers and great fall color. *P. subhirtella* (Higan cherry) is a rounded or spreading tree grown for its white or light pink flowers, attractive bark and bright fall color. *P. x yedoensis* (yoshino cherry) is a large-spreading tree with arching branches and early-spring, pale pink flowers.

Features: upright, rounded, spreading or weeping deciduous tree or shrub; pink, white spring to early-summer flowers; fruit; bark; fall foliage **Height:** 4–75' **Spread:** 4–50' **Hardiness:** zones 2–8

Redbud
Cercis

C. canadensis (above & below)

Tips
Redbud can be used as a specimen tree, in a shrub or mixed border or in a woodland garden.

Recommended
C. canadensis (eastern redbud) is a spreading, multi-stemmed native tree that bears red, purple or pink flowers. The young foliage is bronze to burgundy, fading to green over summer and turning bright yellow in fall. The species grows 30' tall and wide. Many beautiful cultivars are available, including **'Alba'** with white blossoms, and **'Forest Pansy'** bearing dramatic, dark red-purple leaves.

Redbud is an outstanding treasure of early spring. Deep magenta flowers bloom before the leaves emerge, and their impact is intense. As the buds open, the flowers turn pink, covering the long, thin branches in pastel clouds.

Growing
Redbud grows well in **full sun to light shade**. The soil should be a **fertile, deep loam** that is **moist** and **well drained**.

This plant has tender roots and does not like being transplanted.

C. chinensis (Chinese redbud) is a densely branched shrub or small tree with rounded, glossy leaves that turn yellow in fall. Clusters of pink to lavender-pink flowers emerge in spring. This species grows 20' tall and 15' wide. Cultivars are available, including **'Avondale,'** which bears deep purple flowers.

Redbud is not as long-lived as many other trees, so use its delicate beauty to supplement more permanent trees in the garden.

Features: rounded or spreading, multi-stemmed, deciduous tree or shrub; red, purple, pink spring flowers; fall foliage **Height:** 20–30' **Spread:** 15–30' **Hardiness:** zones 4–9

Rhododendron • Azalea

Rhododendron

Even without their flowers, rhododendrons are wonderful landscape plants. Their striking, dark green foliage lends an interesting texture to a shrub planting in summer.

Growing

Rhododendrons prefer **partial shade** or **light shade**, but they tolerate full sun in a site with adequate moisture. A location **sheltered** from strong winds is preferable. The soil should be **fertile, humus rich, acidic, moist** and very **well drained**. Rhododendrons are sensitive to high pH, salinity and winter injury.

Tips

Use rhododendrons and azaleas in shrub or mixed borders, in woodland gardens, as specimen plants, in group plantings, as hedges and informal barriers, in rock gardens or in planters on a shady patio or balcony.

Rhododendrons and azaleas are generally grouped together. Extensive breeding and hybridizing is making it more and more difficult to label them separately.

Recommended

In the Carolinas, we can grow many different rhododendron and azalea species and cultivars. Many wonderful nurseries and specialty growers can help you find the right rhododendrons or azaleas for your garden, based on your height, blooming time and color needs.

The variety 'PJM' is one of the earliest rhododendrons to flower with rich, light purple blooms brightening up the late winter landscape.

Features: upright, mounding, rounded, evergreen or deciduous shrub; late-winter to early-summer flowers in almost every color imaginable; foliage **Height:** 2–12'
Spread: 2–12' **Hardiness:** zones 3–8

River Birch

Betula

B. nigra

When it comes to showy bark, the birch tree is unmatched. As it ages, its attractive, peeling bark adds a whole new dimension to the garden.

Growing

River birch grows well in **full sun, partial shade** or **light shade**. The soil should be of **average to high fertility, moist** and fairly **well drained**. Periodic flooding is tolerated but persistently wet soils will stress these trees.

Tips

Birch trees are often used as specimens. Their small leaves and open canopy provide light shade that allows perennials, annuals and lawns to flourish underneath. If you have enough space in your garden, birches look attractive when grown in groups near natural or artificial water features.

Recommended

B. nigra (river birch) has shaggy, cinnamon brown bark that flakes off in sheets when it is young, but the bark thickens and becomes more ridged as the tree matures. It grows 60–90' tall and spreads 40–60'. This species is more resistant to pests and disease. The cultivar **'Heritage'** has exceptional, light-colored, peeling bark, and **'Summer Cascade'** is a newly introduced weeping form.

B. pendula (European white birch) is a narrowly, conical tree with weeping branches and peeling, white bark. Diamond-shaped, toothed leaves lightly clothe the branches, allowing sunlight to penetrate to the base of the trunk. Many cultivars and hybrids are available. **'Crimson Frost'** is a weeping Asian selection with burgundy leaves, and **'Purple Rain'** bears purple leaves against white bark.

Features: open, deciduous tree; attractive foliage; bark; fall color; winter and spring catkins **Height:** 25–90' **Spread:** 15–60' **Hardiness:** zones 3–8

Rose-of-Sharon

Hibiscus

*I*f you're looking for a tropical look in your backyard, then look no further. Rose-of-Sharon will bring you back to the tropics each summer without even leaving home.

Growing

Rose-of-Sharon prefers **full sun** but tolerates partial shade. It responds well in **fertile** soil that is **humus rich, moist** and **well drained**, but it tolerates poor soil and wet spots.

Pinch young shrubs to encourage bushy growth. Young plants can be trained to form a single-stemmed tree by selectively pruning out all but the strongest stems. The flowers form on the current year's growth; prune back the tip growth in late winter or early spring for larger but fewer flowers.

Tips

Rose-of-Sharon is best used in shrub borders or mixed borders.

This shrub develops unsightly bare branches towards its base as it matures. Plant low, bushy perennials or shrubs around the base to hide them.

The leaves emerge late in spring and drop in early fall. Planting rose-of-Sharon along with evergreen shrubs will make up for its short period of leafiness.

H. syriacus 'Diana' (above)
H. syriacus 'Red Heart' (below)

Recommended

H. syriacus is an erect, multi-stemmed shrub that bears dark pink flowers from mid-summer to fall. Many cultivars are available, including **'Blue Bird'** that bears large, blue flowers with red centers and the **Goddess Series**, bearing big, single, thick, long-lasting flowers in a variety of bright colors.

Features: bushy, upright, vase-shaped, deciduous shrub; mid-summer to fall flowers in solid or bicolored **Height:** 8–12'
Spread: 6–8' **Hardiness:** zones 5–10

Serviceberry

Amelanchier

A. canadensis (above)

Tips

With spring flowers, edible fruit, attractive leaves that turn red in fall and often-artistic branch growth, serviceberries make beautiful specimen plants or even shade trees in small gardens. The shrubbier forms can be grown along the edges of a woodland or in a border. In the wild these trees are often found growing near water sources, and they are beautiful beside ponds or streams.

Recommended

Several species and hybrids are available. A few popular serviceberries are *A. arborea* (downy serviceberry, Juneberry), a small, single- or multi-stemmed tree; 'Autumn Brilliance' offers stunning red fall color; *A. canadensis* (shadblow serviceberry), a large, upright, suckering native shrub; and *A.* x *grandiflora* (apple serviceberry), a small, spreading, often multi-stemmed tree. They all have white flowers, reddish fruit and good fall color.

The *Amelanchier* species are first-rate North American natives, bearing lacy clusters of white flowers in spring, followed by edible berries. In fall the foliage color ranges from a glowing apricot to deep red.

Growing

Serviceberries grow well in **full sun** or **light shade**. They prefer **acidic** soil that is **fertile, humus rich, moist** and **well drained**. They do adjust to drought.

Serviceberry fruit can be used in place of blueberries in any recipe. The fruit has a similar but generally sweeter flavor.

Features: single- or multi-stemmed, deciduous, large shrub or small tree; white spring or early-summer flowers; edible fruit; fall color; bark
Height: 4–30' **Spread:** 4–30'
Hardiness: zones 3–9

Slender Deutzia

Deutzia

$\mathcal{A}$n old-fashioned, frilly lady, the slender deutzia earns only a brief spell in the spotlight when she puts on a fantastic show in spring, covered with a lacy veil of white blossoms for all to see.

Growing

Slender deutzia grows best in **full sun**. It tolerates light shade, but will not bear as many flowers. The soil should be of **average to high fertility, moist** and **well drained**. These shrubs bloom on the previous year's growth.

After flowering, cut flowering stems back to strong buds, main stems or basal growth as required to shape the plant. Remove one-third of the old growth on established plants at ground level to encourage new growth.

Tips

Include deutzias in shrub or mixed borders or in rock gardens. As specimens, they are beautiful in flower but are not too interesting afterward.

Recommended

D. gracilis is a mounding, low-growing species. It produces slender, arching branches that result in a graceful form. In late spring the plant is completely covered with white flowers. A number

D. gracilis (above), D. gracilis hybrid (below)

of cultivars are available in more compact forms and fuller flowers, including **'Nikko,'** a low-growing selection that bears white flowers and dark blue-green foliage that turns burgundy in the fall.

This group of flowering shrubs is known for its tolerance to neglect and extreme conditions.

Features: low-growing, mounding, arching deciduous shrub; white flowers; form
Height: 2–4' **Spread:** 3–6'
Hardiness: zones 5–8

Smoketree
Cotinus

C. coggygria (above & below)

Bright fall color, adaptability, flowers of differing colors, and variable sizes and forms make smoketree and all its cultivars excellent additions to the garden.

Growing

Smoketree grows well in **full sun** or **partial shade**. It prefers soil of **average fertility** that is **moist** and **well drained**, but it adapts to all but very wet soils.

Tips

Smoketree can be used in a shrub or mixed border, as a single specimen or in groups. It is a good choice for a rocky hillside planting.

Recommended

C. coggygria is a bushy, rounded shrub to small tree that develops large, puffy plumes of flowers that start out green and gradually turn a pinky gray. The green foliage turns red, orange and yellow in fall. Many cultivars are available, including purple-leaved varieties like **'Royal Purple'** and the golden-leaved selection **'Golden Spirit.'**

Plant smoketree where you can view sunlight illuminating its colorful leaves and flower plumes.

Features: bushy, rounded, spreading, deciduous tree or shrub; attractive, green flowers turning a pinky gray in early summer; summer and fall foliage **Height:** 10–15' **Spread:** 10–15' **Hardiness:** zones 4–8

Snowbell
Styrax

S. japonica (above & below)

Snowbells are easy to admire for their delicate, shapely appearance and dangling flowers clustered along the undersides of the branches.

Growing

Snowbells grow well in **full sun, partial shade** or **light shade**. The soil should be **fertile, humus rich, neutral to acidic, moist** and **well drained**.

Tips

Snowbells can be used to provide light shade in shrub or mixed borders. They can also be included in woodland gardens, and they make interesting specimens near entryways or patios.

Features: upright, rounded, spreading or columnar, deciduous tree; late-spring to early-summer flowers in pink or white; foliage **Height:** 20–40' **Spread:** 20–30' **Hardiness:** zones 4–8

Recommended

S. americana (American snowbell) is a rounded, native shrub that grows 6–9' tall and a little less wide. It produces zigzagging stems clothed in bright green foliage and fragrant, single, or clusters of nodding, bell-shaped, white flowers in late spring.

S. japonica (Japanese snowbell) is a small, graceful, upright tree. It has arching branches from which white blossoms dangle in late spring. The species grows 25–30' tall and wide. **'Carillon'** is a weeping variety, and **'Emerald Pagoda'** displays a similar habit but at twice the size. **'Pink Chimes'** is slightly more upright in form with pink blossoms.

Spirea
Spiraea

S. *japonica* 'Goldmound' (above), S. x *vanhouttei* (below)

Spireas, seen in so many gardens and with dozens of cultivars, remain undeniable favorites. With a wide range of forms, sizes and colors of both foliage and flowers, spireas have many possible uses in the landscape.

Growing
Spireas prefer **full sun to partial shade**. To help prevent foliage burn, provide protection from very hot sun. The soil should be **fertile, acidic, moist** and **well drained**.

Tips
Spireas are used in shrub or mixed borders, in rock gardens and as informal screens and hedges.

Recommended
Many species, cultivars and hybrids of spirea are available, including **S. *japonica***, an upright, shrubby species that grows 4–6' tall. It bears 8" wide clusters of pink flowers atop the lush green foliage. **S. *nipponica* 'Snowmound'** is a compact, spreading shrub that grows 3–5' tall and wide, with a profusion of white flowers in late spring. **S. *prunifolia*** (bridal wreath spirea) is a larger shrub with graceful, arching branches, bearing small, double, white flowers from base to tip in late winter. **S. x *vanhouttei*** (Vanhoutte spirea) is a dense, bushy shrub with arching branches that bears clusters of white flowers in spring. Check with your local nursery or garden center to see what is available.

Features: round, bushy, deciduous shrub; attractive, summer flowers in white or pink **Height:** 1–10' **Spread:** 1–12' **Hardiness:** zones 3–9

Sweet Mock Orange
Philadelphus

P. coronarius 'Minnesota Snowflake' (above), *P. coronarius* (below)

Grow sweet mock orange if only for its heavenly fragrance, which is reminiscent of orange blossoms.

Growing

Sweet mock oranges grow well in **full sun**, **partial shade** or **light shade**. The soil should be of **average fertility**, **humus rich**, **moist** and **well drained**.

Tips

Include sweet mock oranges in shrub or mixed borders. Use them in groups to create barriers and screens.

Recommended

P. coronarius (sweet mock-orange) is an upright, broadly rounded shrub with fragrant, white flowers. It grows quite tall and wide. Cultivars with variegated or chartreuse foliage are available.

P. x *lemoinei* is a group of hybrids that grow 5–6' tall and wide, bearing clusters of fragrant flowers. Single- or double-flowered cultivars are available.

P. x *virginalis* (virginal mock orange) is an upright, medium-sized shrub. It bears single or double, white flowers later than *P. coronarius*. Cultivars are available with large, double flowers.

Mock oranges combine well with forsythias and reliably produce abundant blooms each year.

Features: rounded, deciduous shrub with arching branches; early-summer, fragrant, white flowers **Height:** 1½–12' **Spread:** 1½–12' **Hardiness:** zones 3–8

Viburnum
Viburnum

V. opulus (above), V. plicatum var. tomentosum (below)

Good fall color, attractive form, shade tolerance, scented flowers and attractive fruit put viburnums in a class by themselves.

Growing
Viburnums grow well in **full sun, partial shade** or **light shade**. The soil should be of **average fertility, moist** and **well drained**. Viburnums tolerate both alkaline and acidic soils.

These plants will look neatest if deadheaded, but this practice will prevent fruits from forming. Fruiting is better when more than one plant of a species is grown.

Tips
Viburnums can be used in borders and woodland gardens. They are a good choice for plantings near swimming pools.

Recommended
Many viburnum species, hybrids and cultivars are available. A few popular ones include *V. carlesii* (Korean spice viburnum), a dense, bushy, rounded, deciduous shrub with white or pink, scented flowers in spring (zones 5–8); *V. dentatum* (arrowwood), a shade-loving, upright shrub with blue fruit (zones 3–7); *V. opulus* (European cranberrybush), a rounded, spreading, cold-tolerant deciduous shrub with lacy-looking flower clusters (zones 3–8); *V. plicatum* var. *tomentosum* (doublefile viburnum), with a graceful, horizontal branching pattern, which gives the shrub a layered effect, and lacy-looking, white flower clusters (zones 5–8); and *V. tinus*, a rounded evergreen that blooms in late winter, but must have protection from winter wind and direct sun.

Features: bushy or spreading, evergreen, semi-evergreen or deciduous shrub; attractive, white, pink flowers (some fragrant); summer and fall foliage; fruit **Height:** 1½–20' **Spread:** 1½–15' **Hardiness:** zones 2–8

Weigela
Weigela

Weigelas have been improved through breeding, and specimens with more compact forms, longer flowering periods and greater cold tolerance are now available.

Growing

Weigela prefers **full sun** but tolerates partial shade. The soil should be **fertile** and **well drained**. This plant adapts to most well-drained soil conditions.

Tips

Weigelas can be used in shrub or mixed borders, in open woodland gardens and as informal barrier plantings.

Recommended

W. florida is a spreading shrub with arching branches that bears clusters of dark pink flowers. Many hybrids and cultivars are available. Some of the best selections include '**Carnaval**,' with red, white or pink, thick, azalea-like flowers; MIDNIGHT WINE, a low-mounding dwarf with dark burgundy foliage; '**Polka**,' with bright pink flowers; '**Red Prince**,' with dark red flowers; '**Rubidor**,' with yellow foliage and red flowers; '**Variegata**,' with yellow-green variegated foliage and pink flowers; and WINE AND ROSES, with dark burgundy foliage and rosy-pink-colored flowers.

W. florida 'Variegata' (above), *W. florida* cultivar (below)

Weigela is one of the longest-blooming shrubs, with the main flush of blooms lasting as long as six weeks. It often re-blooms if sheared lightly after the first flowers fade.

Features: upright or low, spreading, deciduous shrub; late-spring to early-summer flowers in shades of red, white, pink; foliage
Height: 1–9' **Spread:** 1–12'
Hardiness: zones 3–8

Witchhazel

Hamamelis

H. mollis

itchhazel is an investment in happiness. It blooms from late winter through early spring; the flowers last for weeks and their spicy fragrance awakens the senses. Then in fall, the handsome leaves develop overlapping bands of orange, yellow and red.

Growing

Witchhazel grows best in a **sheltered** spot with **full sun** or **light shade**. The soil should be of **average fertility, neutral to acidic, moist** and **well drained**.

Tips

Witchhazels work well individually or in groups. They can be used as specimen plants, in shrub or mixed borders or in woodland gardens. As small trees, they are ideal for space-limited gardens.

Recommended

H. x *intermedia* is a vase-shaped, spreading shrub that bears fragrant clusters of yellow, orange or red flowers. The leaves turn shades of orange, red and bronze in fall. Cultivars with flowers in shades of red, yellow or orange are available, and they include **'Arnold Promise,'** a yellow-flowering selection with fiery fall color; red-flowering **'Diane'**; coppery orange **'Jelena'**; pale yellow **'Primavera'**; and **'Sunburst,'** with heavy clusters of bright yellow flowers and great fall color.

H. mollis (Chinese witchhazel) is a small tree that flowers in the coldest of winter, producing the most fragrant flowers. **'Pallida'** has light yellow flowers.

H. virginiana (common witchhazel) is a native, late-fall-blooming species with an open, spreading form and slow growth habit, and golden yellow, fragrant flowers.

Features: spreading, deciduous shrub or small tree; fragrant, early-spring flowers in fiery shades of yellow, orange, red; attractive summer and fall foliage **Height:** 6–20' **Spread:** 6–20' **Hardiness:** zones 5–8

Carefree Beauty

Modern Shrub · Landscape Rose

This magnificent rose was developed by the late Dr. Griffith J. Buck at Iowa State University. It is one in the long line of Dr. Buck's 'prairie' showstoppers that are perfectly suited to Carolina gardens.

Growing

Carefree Beauty requires a location in **full sun. Well-drained, organically rich, slightly acidic soil** is best, but this shrub rose tolerates slight shade and poorer soils.

Tips

This upright shrub has a spreading habit, which makes it an ideal candidate for a low-maintenance hedge. It also makes a fine specimen, and complements other flowering shrubs and perennials in mixed borders.

Recommended

Rosa **'Carefree Beauty'** bears small clusters of deep pink, 4 $^1/_2$" wide, semi-double blossoms, not once but twice throughout the growing season. The blossoms are large, which balances out the small quantities of flowers produced at the end of each stem. The fragrant flowers beautifully complement the smooth, olive green foliage. Orange-red hips follow after the flowers, adding winter interest to the landscape into the early months of spring.

Carefree Beauty was introduced into the marketplace in 1977. It was the result of crossing an unidentified rose seedling with 'Prairie Princess.'

Features: fragrant, large, deep pink blossoms; disease-free foliage; vigorous growth habit **Height:** 5–6' **Spread:** 4–5' **Hardiness:** zones 3–9

Iceberg
Floribunda Rose

Over 40 years have passed since this exceptional rose was first introduced into commerce, and its continued popularity proves it can stand the test of time.

Growing
Iceberg grows best in **full sun**. The soil should be **fertile, humus rich, slightly acidic, moist** and **well drained**. Winter protection is required. Deadhead to prolong blooming.

Tips
Iceberg is a popular addition to mixed borders and beds, and also works well as a specimen. Plant it in a well-used area or near a window where

its flower fragrance can best be enjoyed. This rose can also be included in large planters or patio containers.

Recommended
Rosa 'Iceberg' is a vigorous shrub with a rounded, bushy habit and light green foliage. It produces clusters of semi-double flowers in several flushes from early summer to fall. A climbing variation of this rose is reputed to be the best climbing white rose ever developed.

Iceberg's profuse blooms almost obscure its foliage. Remove the blooms as they fade to keep the plant blooming until at least the first fall frost.

Also called: fée des neiges **Features:** bushy habit; strong, sweet fragrance; early-summer to fall flowers in white, sometimes flushed with pink during cool or wet weather **Height:** 3–4' **Spread:** 3–4' **Hardiness:** zones 5–8

Knockout

Modern Shrub · Landscape Rose

Knockout (above & below)

This rose is simply one of the best new shrub roses to hit the market in years.

Growing

Knockout grows best in **full sun**. The soil should be **fertile, humus rich, slightly acidic, moist** and **well drained**. This rose blooms most prolifically in warm weather but has deeper red flowers in cooler weather. Deadhead lightly to keep the plant tidy and to encourage prolific blooming.

Tips

This vigorous rose makes a good addition to a mixed bed or border, and it is attractive when planted in groups of three or more. It can be mass planted to create a large display, or grown singly as an equally beautiful specimen.

Recommended

Rosa 'Knockout' has a lovely, rounded form with glossy, green leaves that turn to shades of burgundy in fall. The bright cherry red flowers are borne in clusters of 3–15 almost all summer and into fall. Orange-red hips last well into winter. **'Double Knockout,' 'Pink Knockout'** and a light pink selection called **'Blushing Knockout'** are available. All have excellent disease resistance.

If you've been afraid that roses need too much care, you'll appreciate the hardiness and disease resistance of this low-maintenance beauty.

Features: rounded habit; light, tea-rose scented, mid-summer to fall flowers in shades of pink or red; disease resistant **Height:** 3–4' **Spread:** 3–4' **Hardiness:** zones 4–10

Lady Banks Rose

R. banksiae, Species Rose

*I*t is almost hard to believe your eyes when you first see a mature specimen left to its own devices. Blooming only once, this rose bears a staggering amount of flowers over a six-week period beginning in very early spring.

Growing

Lady Banks Rose will thrive and bloom prolifically in **full to partial sun**. The soil should be **moderately fertile, humus rich, moist** but **very well drained**.

Prune the spent wood only once Lady Banks Rose has finished flowering. It requires little pruning but it's best to stay

Many astonishing claims have been made about this species rose and one holds true: not only does it hold its own with wisteria, but it blooms at the same time, something that most other roses don't do.

on top of it to prevent this rose from taking over small villages. The flowers are produced on second or third year wood.

Tips

The best place to plant this rose is at the base of an old tree, out-building or a location with strong support. It can also be kept to a smaller size with ardent pruning and discipline.

Recommended

R. banksiae is a climbing species rose that produces long, slender stems with little to no prickles and pale green foliage. It bears clusters of double, white or yellow, scented flowers. Cultivars are available, but 'Lutea' is the most popular, bearing fully double, yellow blossoms.

Features: yellow, lightly scented flowers; habit **Height:** 15–20' **Spread:** 15–20' **Hardiness:** zones 5–10

New Dawn

Climbing Rose

Introduced in 1930, New Dawn is still a favorite climbing rose of gardeners and rosarians alike.

Growing
New Dawn grows best in **full sun**. The soil should be **average to fertile, humus rich, slightly acidic, moist** and **well drained**. This rose is disease resistant.

Tips
Train New Dawn to climb pergolas, walls, pillars, arbors, trellises and fences. With some judicious pruning this rose can be trained to form a bushy shrub or hedge. Plant this rose where the springtime profusion of blooms will welcome visitors to your home.

Recommended
Rosa '**New Dawn**' is a vigorous climber and repeat bloomer with upright, arching canes and glossy green foliage. It bears pale pink flowers, singly or in small clusters.

New Dawn was inducted into the World Federation of Rose Societies' Hall of Fame in 1997.

Features: glossy green foliage; climbing habit; long blooming period; pale pearl pink flowers with a sweet, apple-like fragrance
Height: 10–15' **Spread:** 10–15'
Hardiness: zones 4–9

Old Blush
Old Garden Rose

Old Blush was one of four roses that were brought to Europe from China in the mid-1700s. It was used to create many of the modern repeat bloom roses that are so popular today.

Growing
Old Blush grows well in **full to partial sun**. The soil should be **fertile, well drained** and **humus rich**.

Tips
This small rose bush would be stunning toward the front of a mixed shrub border or within a rose garden. The sweet-pea-scented blossoms are best enjoyed near pathways, balconies, patios and windows.

Recommended
R. **'Old Blush'** is an upright, bushy shrub with a moderately vigorous growth habit. This China rose is resistant to disease and produces smooth canes with few thorns. The glossy leaves are produced in abundance. Medium pink, semi-double to double blossoms are produced in early spring and may repeat bloom later in the season.

Also called: Common Blush China, Monthly Rose, Parson's Pink China **Features:** lightly fragrant, pink flowers; disease resistance
Height: 3–4' **Spread:** 3'
Hardiness: zones 7–9

Queen Elizabeth

Grandiflora Rose

The grandiflora classification was originally created to accommodate this rose. Queen Elizabeth is one of the most widely grown and best-loved roses.

Growing

Queen Elizabeth grows best in **full sun**. The soil should be **average to fertile, humus rich, slightly acidic, moist** and **well drained**, but this durable rose adapts to most soils and tolerates high heat and humidity. Prune plants back to 5–7 canes and 5–7 buds each spring.

Tips

Queen Elizabeth is a trouble-free rose that makes a good addition to mixed borders and beds. It can also be used as a specimen, to form a hedge or in a large planter. Its flowers are borne on sturdy stems that make them useful for floral arrangements.

Recommended

Rosa 'Queen Elizabeth' is a bushy shrub with glossy, dark green foliage and dark stems. The pink, cup-shaped, double flowers may be borne singly or in clusters.

Queen Elizabeth has won many honors and was named World's Favorite Rose in 1979.

Features: glossy, dark green, disease-resistant foliage; soft, pearly pink, lightly scented, summer to fall flowers **Height:** 4–6'
Spread: 30–36" **Hardiness:** zones 5–9

The Fairy

Modern Shrub Rose

The Fairy is popular with novice and experienced gardeners alike. It bears large clusters of dainty, soft pink, rosette-shaped, double flowers.

Growing

The Fairy grows well in **full sun or partial shade**, in **fertile, moist, well-drained soil** with at least **5% organic matter** mixed in. It is prone to blackspot when planted in partial shade but will still bloom.

Roses can tolerate light breezes, but keep them out of strong winds. These heavy feeders and drinkers do not like to share their root space with other plants.

This rose doesn't just tolerate neglect, it prefers it. It manages successfully in partial shade, and this slows the fading of the flower color.

Tips

This rose can be used in containers, as groundcovers, in mixed beds and borders, as a weeping standard, or it can be left to trail over a low wall or embankment. It looks great massed or planted as low hedging. It also makes a beautiful cut flower.

Recommended

Rosa **'The Fairy'** is a compact-mounding plant with moderately prickly canes and glossy foliage. It is trouble free and moderately resistant to disease. It blooms continually until fall frost.

Features: repeat blooming; soft pink late-summer to fall flowers; low maintenance
Height: 24–36" **Spread:** 24–36"
Hardiness: zones 4–9

Carolina Jessamine

Gelsemium

Most Carolinians are familiar with this flowering vine. It's known to scamper up large trees, fences and even utility poles. Golden yellow flowers adorn this sprawling vine in late winter, reminding us that spring is just around the corner.

Growing

Carolina Jessamine thrives in locations with **full sun**. It will grow in partial shade but produces fewer flowers. The soil should be **moist, well drained** and **fertile**.

Pinch back the new growth to encourage a more dense growth habit. Cut it back to approximately 2–3' high when the growth is thin at the bottom and the top is falling over because of the weight.

Tips

This vine can be grown on a decorative trellis, pergola or an arbor. It climbs by twining or wrapping itself around a support. It is often used to adorn mailboxes and just about anything that requires a bit of color and a vertical element.

All parts of this plant are **poisonous**.

Recommended

G. sempervirens is a vigorous, native vine that produces twining stems without the aid of tendrils. Masses of fragrant, funnel-shaped flowers are borne in late winter in shades of golden to pale yellow. Dark, glossy, evergreen foliage on rich brown stems is the perfect complement to the brightly colored blossoms.

G. sempervirens (above & below)

This vine can also be used as an effective groundcover when maintained. Plant in a place where it can be left to roam and won't be bothered once established.

Features: bright yellow flower clusters; lush foliage and habit **Height:** 15–20'
Spread: 4–5' **Hardiness:** zones 7–9

Clematis

Clematis

C. 'Etoile Violette' (above), C. 'Gravetye Beauty' (below)

There are so many species, hybrids and cultivars of clematis that it is possible to have one in bloom all season.

Growing

Clematis plants prefer **full sun** but tolerate partial shade. The soil should be **fertile, humus rich, moist** and **well drained**. These vines enjoy warm, sunny weather, but the roots prefer to be cool. A thick layer of mulch or a planting of low, shade-providing perennials will protect the tender roots. The rootball of vining clematis should be planted about 2" beneath the surface of the soil.

It is important to know the pruning time preferred by your clematis as they differ depending on the type. Most of the herbaceous clematis should be cut back after hard frost.

Tips

Clematis vines can climb up structures such as trellises, railings, fences and arbors. They can also be allowed to grow over shrubs and up trees and can be used as groundcover.

Recommended

There are many species, hybrids and cultivars of clematis. The flower forms, blooming times and sizes of the plants can vary and are available in just about every form and color imaginable. Check with your local garden center to see what is available.

Plant two clematis varieties together that bloom at the same time to provide a mix of color and texture, or allow one to run through your climbing roses.

Features: twining habit; blue, purple, pink, yellow, red, white early to late-summer flowers; decorative seedheads **Height:** 10–17' or more **Spread:** 5' or more **Hardiness:** zones 3–8

Climbing Hydrangea
Hydrangea

Climbing hydrangea is an attractive vine that is ideal to grow up and through tall specimen trees. Trees provides a structure to climb, and the tree's foliage helps shade the vine.

Growing

Climbing hydrangea grows best in **partial shade** in **humus-rich, moist, well-drained, acidic** soil of **average fertility**. It adapts to more sun and to most soils as long as the soil remains moist. It appreciates **shelter** from the hot afternoon sun and from strong or drying winds.

Once established, prune out overly aggressive growth.

Tips

Climbing hydrangea is used as a climbing vine and also as a groundcover. It clings to structures and to flat surfaces such as walls by use of aerial rootlets. It will slowly cover walls and arbors, and truly anything else it is close to. The attractive, peeling bark provides winter interest.

Recommended

H. anomala subsp. *petiolaris* is a vigorous, woody climber. The stems 'cling' by aerial roots or holdfasts. The foliage is reminiscent of other hydrangea species, and the flower clusters are very similar in appearance

H. anomala subsp. *petiolaris* (above & below)

to lacecap hydrangea (*H. macrophylla*), bearing flattened clusters of insignificant, fertile flowers, which are surrounded by open, infertile flowers in creamy white.

The lacecap flower cluster or inflorescence can grow 6–10" in width.

Features: attractive foliage and bark; white summer flowers; habit **Height:** 40' or more when climbing; shrubby and sprawling without support **Spread:** dependent on support **Hardiness:** zones 5–9

Cross Vine

Bignonia

B. capreolata 'Jeckyll' (above & below)

This native vine is known to grow very large and at a rapid rate. It blooms like crazy in early spring and will disguise unsightly surfaces and structures in no time.

Growing

Cross vine can tolerate a wide range of soil conditions but prefers **organically rich, well-drained, moist** soil in **full sun**. Partial sun is tolerated but cross vine may flower less.

Prune after flowering and when you find it necessary to train it on its support.

Tips

This twining plant will climb up just about anything. The stems climb by little suction cup-like bits at the end of their tendrils and rootlets called holdfast disks. When first planted, this vine will need to be attached to the surface or structure it will eventually climb. Any type of garden structure will work, along with stone or brick walls, fences, poles and trees.

Recommended

B. capreolata is a twining, semi-evergreen, vigorous vine that produces lush, green foliage on long, tough stems. Orange-yellow, tubular flowers with reddish throats emerge in spring. The foliage takes on a purplish red color as the days grow cooler in winter. Cultivars are available in other fiery colors as well.

Cross vine is sometimes confused with trumpet creeper. Although they look somewhat similar, cross vine doesn't have the same invasive nature and blooms at a different time throughout the growing season.

Features: bright, fiery-colored flowers; vigorous twining habit **Height:** 30–50' **Spread:** 20–40' **Hardiness:** zones 6–9

Evergreen Wisteria
Millettia

M. reticulata (above & below)

This twining, woody climber is known as evergreen wisteria for its lasting, lush foliage. Evergreen wisteria is a fine substitute for true wisteria, as it doesn't grow as large or aggressively but is equally as stunning.

Growing
Evergreen wisteria grows well in **full sun or light shade**. The soil should be **well drained** and **moderately fertile**.

Tips
Evergreen wisteria is ideal for a strong trellis or support. The rope-like, woody stems, and the blooms reminiscent of wisteria, are best displayed on a pergola, gazebo or arbor.

Recommended
M. reticulata (evergreen wisteria, summer wisteria) is a vigorous, twining vine that produces shiny, leathery leaves, divided into many leaflets. Tight clusters of deep purple-red flowers emerge in late summer. The flowers are mildly fragrant, with a camphor-like aroma.

This species of Millettia *is evergreen in tropical, coastal areas of the southern U.S. but deciduous throughout the cooler inland areas.*

Features: purple-red, wisteria-like flowers; shiny foliage; vigorous habit **Height:** 15–20'
Spread: 6–10' **Hardiness:** zones 7–10

Ipomoea

Ipomoea

I. batatas 'Margarita' (above), *I. tricolor* (below)

Vines within this group are incredibly easy to grow and are bound to make even the beginner feel like an expert.

Growing

Ipomoea prefers **full sun** and a **light, well-drained** soil of **poor fertility** but any type of soil will do. Soak seeds for 24 hours before sowing. Start seeds in individual peat pots if sowing indoors. Plant in late spring after the last expected frost date.

Tips

Sweet potato vine is a great addition to mixed planters, window boxes and hanging baskets. In a rock garden it will scramble about, and along the top of a retaining wall it will cascade over the edge.

Recommended

I. *alba* (moonflower) has sweet-scented, white flowers that open at night.

I. *batatas* (sweet potato vine) is a twining climber that is grown for its attractive foliage rather than its flowers. Several cultivars are available.

I. *purpurea* (common morning glory) bears trumpet-shaped flowers in purple, blue, pink or white that close in the heat of the day.

I. *quamoclit* (Cypress vine) is an annual vine with finely divided, dark green foliage and scarlet red, starry-shaped flowers. This species can grow to 20' in height.

I. x *sloteri* (syn. *I.* x *multifida*, cardinal climber) is a slender, twining annual vine with numerous, small, crimson red flowers and broad, 4 ¹/₂" wide leaves divided into sharply pointed segments.

I. *tricolor* (morning glory) produces purple or blue flowers with white centers. Many cultivars are available.

Features: colorful, decorative foliage; fast growth; white, blue, pink or purple and variegated flowers **Height:** 1–12' **Spread:** 1–10' **Hardiness:** annual

Passion Vine
Passiflora

Passion vines are mesmerizing. Most are native to North America.

Growing

Grow passion vine in **full sun** or **partial shade**. It prefers **well-drained, moist** soil of **average fertility**. Keep it **sheltered** from wind and cold.

Passion vine is a fast-growing woody climber that is grown as an annual in the colder parts of the Carolinas. It should thrive for years next to a house without any winter protection in zone 7 and above.

Tips

Passion vine is a popular addition to mixed containers and makes an unusual focal point near a door or other entryway.

Many garden centers sell passion vines in spring, and the vines quickly climb trellises and other supports over summer. They can be composted at the end of summer or cut back and brought inside over winter.

Recommended

P. caerulea (blue passion flower) bears unusual, purple-banded, purple-white flowers all summer. The species can reach 30' heights. **'Constance Elliott'** bears fragrant, white flowers with pale blue or white filaments.

P. caerulea

P. incarnata (maypops) is a vigorous, native, climbing vine, similar to *P. caerulea*, that produces tendrils to attach itself to a support. It has deeply lobed, ornate foliage and bears bowl-shaped, fragrant, pale purple to nearly white blossoms with purple and white coronas which are followed by yellow fruit. This species can reach more than 6' heights.

Features: exotic flowers with white or pale pink petals with blue or purple bands; habit; foliage **Height:** 6–30' **Spread:** variable **Hardiness:** zones 6–10

Purple Hyacinth Bean
Lablab (Dolichos)

L. purpureus (above & below)

With purple hyacinth bean plants and six to eight 6' bamboo poles, you can create a living teepee, a perfect hiding place for a child. It's sure to bring a smile to a child's face.

Growing
Purple hyacinth bean prefers **full sun**. The soil should be **fertile, moist** and **well drained**.

Tips
Purple hyacinth bean needs a trellis, net, pole or other structure to twine up. Plant it against a fence or near a balcony. If you grow it as a groundcover, make sure it doesn't engulf smaller plants.

Recommended
L. purpureus (*Dolichos lablab*) is a vigorous, twining annual vine. It grows up to 30' tall and bears many purple or white flowers over the summer, followed by deep purple pods.

The raw beans contain a cyanide-releasing chemical, so never eat the beans unless they are thoroughly cooked. The purple pods are edible if thoroughly cooked with two to four changes of water.

Also called: Egyptian bean, Lablab bean, Lablab, Indian bean **Features:** large, bold leaves; habit; purple and white sweet-pea-like flowers; also grown for purple pods **Height:** 10–15' **Spread:** variable **Hardiness:** grown as an annual

Trumpet Honeysuckle
Lonicera

Trumpet honeysuckles can be rampant twining vines, but with careful consideration and placement they won't over-run your garden. The fragrance of the flowers makes any effort worthwhile.

Growing

Trumpet honeysuckles grow well in **full sun** or **partial shade**. The soil should be **average to fertile, humus rich, moist** and **well drained**.

Tips

Trumpet honeysuckle can be trained to grow up a trellis, fence, arbor or other structure. In a large container near a porch it will ramble over the edges of the pot and up the railings with reckless abandon.

Recommended

There are many native honey-suckle species, hybrids and culti-vars. Check with your local garden center to see what is available. The following are some of the more popular selections.

L. *sempervirens* (above)
L. x *brownii* 'Dropmore Scarlet' (below)

L. x *brownii* 'Dropmore Scarlet' is one of the hardiest of the climbing honey-suckles, cold hardy to zone 4. It bears bright red flowers for most of summer.

L. *flava* (yellow honeysuckle) is a native vine with yellowish flowers and rounded leaves with a blue cast.

L. *sempervirens* (trumpet honey-suckle, coral honeysuckle) is a native vine that bears orange or red, tubular flowers in late winter through spring and sporadically throughout summer. Many cultivars and hybrids are available with yellow flowers, such as **'John Clayton,'** or red or scarlet flowers, including **'Cedar Lane'** and **'Superba.'**

The flower color and shape is very attractive to hummingbirds and butterflies.

Features: yellow, orange, red, scarlet flowers; twining habit; fruit **Height:** 6–20' **Spread:** 6–20' **Hardiness:** zones 5–9

Virginia Creeper • Boston Ivy
Parthenocissus

P. quinquefolia (above & below)

Virginia creeper and Boston ivy are handsome vines that establish quickly and provide an air of age and permanence, even on new structures.

Growing

These deciduous vines grow well in any light, from **full sun to full shade**. The soil should be **fertile** and **well drained**. The plants adapt to clay or sandy soils.

Tips

Virginia creeper and Boston ivy can cover an entire building, given enough time. They do not require support because they have clinging rootlets that can adhere to just about any surface. They thrive on brick walls but will also climb smooth wood, vinyl or metal surfaces. Give the plants a lot of space and let them cover a wall, fence or arbor.

Recommended

These two species are very similar, except for the shape of the leaves.

P. quinquefolia (Virginia creeper, woodbine) is a native vine that has dark green foliage. Each leaf, divided into five leaflets, turns flame red in fall.

P. tricuspidata (Boston ivy, Japanese creeper) has dark green, three-lobed leaves that turn bright red in fall. This species is not quite as hardy as Virginia creeper. (Zones 4–9)

Features: summer and fall foliage; clinging habit **Height:** 30–70' **Spread:** 30–70' **Hardiness:** zones 3–9

Arum

Arum

This shade-loving plant will provide you with seasonal interest from early fall through the coldest months of winter and into spring.

Growing

Arum grows well in locations with **partial shade** with **shelter** from the afternoon sun. Large leaves will form in a partially shaded location, whereas more sun is required for arum to flower well. The soil should be **humus rich** and **well drained**. Mulch once the leaves have emerged. Divide only when flowering decreases.

Tips

Arum is often planted as an under-story plant. It's also useful and quite lovely in shady perennial borders when planted with other ornamental foliage plants that glow in the shade.

Plant the tubers in fall, a few weeks prior to the first hard frost. They should be planted at least 3" deep and 12" apart.

Recommended

A. ***italicum*** is a tuberous perennial with spear-shaped, dark to medium green leaves veined in white that are showy from fall through spring. In spring, pale greenish white flowers emerge, called spathes. The spathes are then followed by bright orange-red berries that last until new foliage begins to develop. **'Pictum'** produces leaves that are narrower than the species, with cream-colored veins.

A. italicum cultivar (above), *A. italicum* (below)

Arum is the perfect companion plant for hostas; arum rouses from its summer sleep while the hostas are going dormant.

Features: ornate foliage; white spathes; orange-red fruit **Height:** 12–20" **Spread:** 12–24" **Hardiness:** zones 6–9

Canna Lily

Canna

C. 'Red King Humbert' (above & below)

Canna lilies are stunning and dramatically large foliage plants that give an exotic flair to any garden.

Growing

Canna lilies grow best in **full sun** in a **sheltered** location. The soil should be **fertile, moist** and **well drained**. Plant out in spring after the chance of frost has passed and once the soil has warmed. Plants can be started early indoors in containers to get a head start on the growing season. Deadhead to prolong blooming.

Tips

Canna lilies can be grown in a bed or border. They make dramatic specimen plants and can even be included in large planters.

Canna lilies are cold hardy up through zone 7; otherwise, the rhizomes can be lifted after the foliage is killed back in fall. Clean off any clinging dirt and store them in a cool, frost-free location in slightly moist peat moss. Check on them regularly through the winter and if they start to sprout, pot them and move them to a bright window until they can be moved outdoors.

Recommended

A wide range of canna lilies are available, including cultivars and hybrids with green, bronze, purple or yellow-and-green-striped foliage. Dwarf cultivars that only grow 18–28" tall are also available.

Features: decorative foliage; white, red, orange, pink, yellow, bicolored summer flowers **Height:** 3–6' **Spread:** 20–36" **Hardiness:** zones 7–9

Chinese Ground Orchid

Bletilla

B. striata (above & below)

Chinese ground orchid is one of the wonderful surprises that you may encounter in flower this spring.

Growing
Chinese ground orchid grows well in **sheltered locations** with **partial shade**. The soil should be **moist**, very **well drained** and **humus rich**. Mulch around the base to conserve moisture.

Chinese ground orchids can be divided in early spring.

Tips
Woodland gardens are the perfect setting for this plant. Because it requires shelter and shade, plantings under lath houses, pergolas and understories are ideal to ensure it is protected from any extremes. It can also be used for naturalizing under the canopy of trees.

Recommended
B. striata is a terrestrial orchid that bears long, wide, blade-like leaves from the base that emerge from a flattened pseudobulb. Magenta, pendulous flowers poke through the strap-like foliage on wiry stems. Flower colors in white, cream or pale yellow are also available.

Features: magenta, white, cream, pale yellow, spring to early-summer flowers; rich foliage Height: 12–24" Spread: 12–24" Hardiness: zones 5–8

Daffodil

Narcissus

Many gardeners automatically think of large, yellow, trumpet-shaped flowers when they think of daffodils, but there is a lot of variety in color, form and size among the daffodils.

Growing

Daffodils grow best in **full sun** or **light, dappled shade**. The soil should be **average to fertile, moist** and **well drained**. Bulbs should be planted in fall, 2–8" deep, depending on the size of the bulb. The bigger the bulb, the deeper it should be planted. A rule of thumb is to measure the bulb from top to bottom and multiply that number by three to know how deeply to plant.

Tips

Daffodils are often planted where they can be left to naturalize, in the light shade beneath a tree or in a woodland garden. In mixed beds and borders, the faded leaves are hidden by the summer foliage of other plants.

Recommended

Many species, hybrids and cultivars of daffodils are available. Flowers range from 1½–6" across and can be solitary or borne in clusters. There are 13 divisions based on flower-form and heritage categories.

The cup in the center of a daffodil is called the corona, and the group of petals that surrounds the corona is called the perianth.

Features: spring flowers in white, yellow, peach, orange, pink, bicolored **Height:** 4–24" **Spread:** 4–12" **Hardiness:** zones 3–9

Elephant's Ear
Colocasia

Bold foliage is this plant's claim to fame, and bold it is. There are few others that have the same visual impact as this southern favorite.

Growing

Elephant's ear prefers to grow in locations with **partial shade**. The soil should be **moist to wet**, **slightly acidic, humus rich** and very **fertile**.

Plant bulbs blunt end down beneath 2" of soil, and approximately 1–1½' apart. Locations sheltered from strong winds are best, to prevent the leaves from becoming torn and tattered.

Elephant's ear is not completely winter hardy north of zone 8, so you may choose to lift the bulbs in fall for storage.

Tips

Elephant's ear is stunning when planted in large decorative containers surrounded by plants that will spill over the edges. It is also effective when mixed with narrow or finely leaved plants in mixed beds and borders.

Recommended

C. esculenta is a perennial that bears very large, arrow-shaped, dark green leaves supported by stalks up to 3' long. Flowers rarely appear. Cultivars are available with dark red, purple, light green or blackish purple stalks and veins.

C. esculenta (above)

C. esculenta *is a marginal aquatic perennial, which means it thrives in wet conditions, including near water features and bog gardens.*

Features: bold foliage; form **Height:** 5–8'
Spread: 5–8' **Hardiness:** zones 9–11

Grape Hyacinth
Muscari

M. botryoides (above), M. armeniacum (below)

Tips

This bulb is great for naturalizing. Plant individual bulbs random distances from one another in lightly wooded areas and mixed borders. They are also quite beautiful planted alongside perennials that will begin to envelope the tired-looking grape hyacinth foliage as they reach their full size. The leaves of grape hyacinth emerge in fall and are often planted around other bulbs and hostas as markers to ensure that these other bulbs aren't forgotten about.

Recommended

M. armeniacum (Armenian grape hyacinth) produces grass-like foliage and clusters of purple-blue, grape-like flowers atop slender, green stems. The flowers emit a strong, musky scent. **'Blue Spike'** produces double, blue flowers, and **'Heavenly Blue'** has sky blue flowers. **'Valerie Finnis'** is the best of all, bearing silvery blue flowers.

M. botryoides (common grape hyacinth) has a form that is slightly more compact. It is less aggressive than other species and will naturalize in a more respectable manner. It bears flowers in blue, pink or white.

affodils should never be alone to signal the emergence of spring. Grape hyacinth bulbs are the perfect accompaniment and contrast beautifully with just about any color combination.

Growing

Grape hyacinth prefers **full sun to partial shade**. The soil should be **well drained** and **organically rich**.

Features: grape-like clusters of fragrant, blue flowers; habit **Height:** 6–10" **Spread:** 6–8" **Hardiness:** zones 2–8

Hardy Cyclamen

Cyclamen

These diminutive plants make a lovely addition to shade gardens where their attractively patterned foliage and winter flowers in shades of pink or white provide interest in a season dominated by evergreens.

Growing

Hardy cyclamen grows best in **light or partial shade**. The soil should be **fertile, humus rich** and extremely **well drained**. Plant hardy cyclamen almost on top of the soil underneath protective trees and overhangs. Add a thin layer of compost to the soil each spring.

Tips

Hardy cyclamen is an attractive plant to use in shaded beds, borders, rock gardens and woodland gardens. It can be used in containers, but may need winter protection because the root temperature fluctuates more in containers.

Recommended

C. coum is a tuberous perennial. It produces rounded leaves that are sometimes shiny and can be unmarked or marked with deep green and silver patterns. The flowers rise above the foliage but remain compact and are borne in white to shades of pink and red. This species grows 2–3" tall.

C. hederifolium forms a low clump of triangular to heart-shaped evergreen foliage. The dark green foliage is patterned with light green and silvery

C. hederifolium (above & below)

markings. Pink or white flowers are produced in fall and late winter. Plants may go dormant during the heat of summer.

Hardy cyclamen can be planted or started in two ways: seed or tubers. Most types of tubers should be planted 6–10" apart and 1/2" deep. Plants grown from seed can take 7–24 months to bloom.

Features: attractive evergreen foliage; pink or white fall flowers **Height:** 4–6" **Spread:** 6–8" **Hardiness:** zones 5–9

Iris
Iris

I. sibirica (above), *I. germanica* 'Stepping Out' (below)

Irises are steeped in history and lore. Many say the flower color range of bearded irises approximates that of a rainbow.

Growing
Irises prefer **full sun** but tolerate very light or dappled shade. The soil should be of **average fertility** and **well drained**.

Japanese iris and Siberian iris prefer a moist but still well-drained soil.

Tips
All irises are popular border plants. Dwarf cultivars make attractive additions to rock gardens.

Wash your hands after handling irises because they can cause severe internal irritation if ingested. You may not want to plant them close to places where babies play.

Recommended
There are many species and hybrids available. Among the most popular is the bearded iris, often a hybrid of *I. germanica*. It has the widest range of flower colors. *I. cristata* (dwarf crested iris) is a low-growing native species that bears multi-colored blossoms. *I. fulva* (copper iris) and *I. virginica* (Virginia iris) both love moisture. *I. pseudoacorus* (yellow flag iris) is a water dweller and tolerates wet locations where little else thrives. *I. sibirica* (Siberian iris) offers assorted cultivars with flowers in a variety of shades, including purple, blue or white. *I. tectorum* (Japanese rooftop iris) produces violet blue with white flowers.

Features: spring, summer and, sometimes, fall flowers in almost every color combination, including bicolored or multi-colored; attractive foliage **Height:** 4"–4' **Spread:** 6"–4' **Hardiness:** zones 3–10

Jack-in-the-Pulpit
Arisaema

*I*f you've ever thought that you'd really like something totally different in your shade garden, then look no further. This curious plant has so much to offer and is certain to please.

Growing

Jack-in-the-pulpit thrives in **partial to full shade**. The soil should be **moist** and **well drained**, **neutral to acidic** and **humus rich**.

The tubers should be planted in fall, approximately 1' apart and 2" deep. The plants will die back down to the ground in winter.

Tips

Jack-in-the-pulpit's preference for humus-rich soils, dappled shade and moisture make it the perfect woodland plant. Planting it under the canopy of larger trees is best, but a standard shade bed is also suitable.

Recommended

A. triphyllum is a tuberous perennial that bears medium to large umbrella-like leaflets that protect the unusual flowers underneath. Green-hooded spathes with purple stripes emerge in spring or early summer. The spathe begins to wither as the flowers are spent. Orange to red seeds follow.

Arisaema is a relative of the calla lily or the genus Zantedeschia in the Arum family.

Features: unusual spathe and flowers; lush foliage **Height:** 2' **Spread:** 1½' **Hardiness:** zones 5–9

Lily
Lilium

L. Asiatic Hybrids (above), L. 'Stargazer' (below)

Decorative clusters of large, richly colored blooms grace these tall plants. Flowers are produced at different times of the season, depending on the hybrid, and it is possible to have lilies blooming all season if a variety of cultivars are chosen.

Growing
Lilies grow best in **full sun** but like to have their **roots shaded**. The soil should be rich in **organic matter, fertile, moist** and **well drained**.

Tips
Lilies are often grouped in beds and borders and can be naturalized in woodland gardens and near water features. These plants are tall but narrow; plant at least three lilies together to create some volume.

Recommended
The many species, hybrids and cultivars available are grouped by type. Visit your local garden center to see what is available. The following are two popular groups of lilies. **Asiatic hybrids** bear clusters of flowers in late spring to early summer and are available in a wide range of colors. **Oriental hybrids** bear clusters of large, fragrant, white, pink or red flowers in mid- and late summer.

L. formosanum (Formosa lily) is known as possibly the easiest lily to grow. It grows extremely tall, bearing white, trumpet-shaped flowers in late summer. They are known to freely reseed themselves.

Lily bulbs are usually planted in fall around the first frost but can also be planted in spring if bulbs are available.

Features: early-, mid- or late-season flowers in shades of orange, yellow, peach, pink, purple, red, white **Height:** 24"–5' **Spread:** 12" **Hardiness:** zones 4–8

Magic Lily

Lycoris

L. squamigera (above), *L. radiata* (below)

Despite its magical appearance, this perennial is also known as the spider lily, based on the outstretched stamens that resemble the legs of an arachnid. It's also known by other names equally as interesting, including surprise lily, hurricane lily, naked lady and the resurrection lily.

Growing

Magic lily prefers to grow in locations with **full sun**. **Fertile, well-drained** soil is best. Mulching is recommended for moisture conservation.

The bulbs are best planted in late summer, about 1' apart. The bulb necks should be just above the soil surface. It's important to select an area for planting that will remain fairly dry during the bulbs' summer dormancy to prevent rot. Some water is tolerated if excellent drainage is available. Propagation by division should only take place once magic lily has stopped blooming for the season.

Tips

Magic lily is ideal for sunny borders and rock gardens.

Recommended

L. radiata (spider lily, hurricane lily) is a bulbous perennial with wavy, deep red flowers. This species grows 12–20" tall and is hardy in zones 8–10.

L. squamigera is a cold-hardy, bulbous perennial that forms clusters of funnel-shaped, pale rosy red flowers made up of slightly wavy petals with curved tips. Long, wiry stamens emerge from the center of each fragrant flower. Strap-shaped leaves are produced each spring.

Features: unique, pinky red flowers; form
Height: 18–24" **Spread:** 12–18"
Hardiness: zones 6–10

Spanish Squill
Hyacinthoides

H. hispanica culitvar (above), *H. hispanica* (below)

This genus of spring-blooming bulbs has experienced several name changes over the years, so don't be surprised to find it under a variety of botanical and common names. Spanish squill is the best choice for southern gardens for its heat tolerance and prolific habit.

Growing

Spanish squill grows in full sun but performs well in **partial shade to deep shade**. The soil should be **rich** and **sandy** but Spanish squill tolerates a wide variety of soils as long as they are very **well drained**, and it has adequate moisture in the spring.

Plant the bulbs soon after purchase as they do not store well and may dry out. The bulbs should be planted at least 3" deep and 1–2" apart from one another.

Tips

Spanish squill is most effective when planted in large groupings. It is ideal for areas that require a subtle touch of blue springtime color. This flowering bulb can also be planted underneath deciduous shrubs for early spring interest. Naturalized areas benefit from random plantings of Spanish squill, adding a hint of color in a meadow-like setting.

Recommended

H. **hispanica** (syn *S. campanulata; S. hispanica*) produces blue, bell-shaped, nodding flowers on 12–16" tall stems rising through strap-like foliage. **'Excelsior'** is an old-fashioned cultivar with dark blue flowers, **'Queen of Pinks'** bears pale pink flowers, and **'White City'** has white flowers.

Also called: Spanish bluebell, wood hyacinth
Features: white, blue, pink flowers; habit; hardiness; tolerance of poor conditions and shade **Height:** 12–24" **Spread:** 24–36"
Hardiness: zones 4–10

Chives
Allium

$\mathcal{T}$he delicate onion flavor of chives is best enjoyed fresh. Mix chives into dips or sprinkle them on salads and baked potatoes.

Growing
Chives grow best in **full sun**. The soil should be **fertile, moist** and **well drained**, but chives adapt to most soil conditions. These plants are easy to start from seed, but they do like the soil temperature to stay above 65° F before they will germinate, so seeds started directly in the garden are unlikely to sprout before early summer.

Chives will spread with reckless abandon as the clumps grow larger and the plants self-seed.

Tips
Chives are decorative enough to be included in a mixed or herbaceous border and can be left to naturalize. In an herb garden, chives should be given plenty of space to allow self-seeding.

Recommended
A. schoenoprasum forms a clump of bright green, cylindrical leaves. Clusters of pinky purple flowers are produced in early and mid-summer. Varieties with white or pink flowers are available.

A. schoenoprasum (above & below)

Chives are said to increase appetite and encourage good digestion.

Features: foliage; form; white, pink, pinky purple flowers **Height:** 8–24"
Spread: 12" or more **Hardiness:** zones 3–9

Fennel
Foeniculum

F. vulgare 'Purpureum' (above & below)

Growing

Fennel grows best in **full sun**. The soil should be **average to fertile, moist** and **well drained**. Avoid planting near dill and coriander as cross-pollination reduces seed production and the seed flavor of each becomes less distinct.

Tips

Fennel is an attractive addition to a mixed bed or border. It can be included in a vegetable garden and does well in any sunny location. It also attracts pollinators and predatory insects to the garden. To collect seeds remove the seed-bearing stems before the seeds start to fall off.

Recommended

F. vulgare is a short-lived perennial that forms clumps of loose, feathery foliage. Clusters of small yellow flowers are borne in late summer. Seeds ripen in fall. A large edible bulb forms at the stem base of the biennial **var.** *azoricum*. The bulb is eaten raw in salads, cooked in soups and stews and roasted like other root vegetables. **'Purpureum'** is similar in appearance to the species but has bronzy purple foliage.

All parts of fennel are edible and have a distinctive licorice-like fragrance and flavor. The seeds are commonly used to make a tea which is good for settling the stomach after a large meal.

Fennel was used for its medicinal and culinary properties before ancient Greek times.

Features: attractive, fragrant foliage; flowers; seeds; stems **Height:** 2–6' **Spread:** 12–24" **Hardiness:** zones 4–9

Mint

Mentha

The cool, refreshing flavor of mint lends itself to tea and other hot or cold beverages. Mint sauce, made from freshly chopped mint leaves, is often served with lamb.

Growing

Mint grows well in **full sun** or **partial shade**. The soil should be **average to fertile, humus rich** and **moist**. These plants spread vigorously by rhizomes and may need a barrier in the soil to restrict their spread.

Tips

Mint is an aggressive groundcover for damp spots. It grows along ditches that may only be periodically wet. It also can be used in beds and borders, but place mint carefully because it may overwhelm less vigorous plants. Mint is really best when grown in a restrictive container.

The flowers attract bees, butterflies and other pollinators to the garden.

Recommended

There are many attractive species, hybrids and cultivars of mint. Spearmint (***M. spicata***), peppermint (***M.* x *piperita***) and orange mint (***M.* x *piperita citrata***) are three of the most commonly grown culinary varieties. Chocolate mint (***M.* x *piperita piperita***) is a unique selection. The flavor is reminiscent of a chocolate mint candy and is useful in desserts

M. x *piperata* 'Chocolate' (above)
M. x *gracilis* 'Variegata' (decorative cultivar; below)

and specialty drinks. There are also more decorative varieties with variegated or curly leaves, as well as varieties with unusual, fruit-scented leaves.

A few sprigs of fresh mint added to a pitcher of iced tea give it an extra zip.

Features: fragrant foliage; purple, pink, white summer flowers **Height:** 6–36"
Spread: 36" or more **Hardiness:** zones 4–8

Oregano • Marjoram
Origanum

O. vulgare 'Aureum' (above & below)

Growing

Oregano and marjoram grow best in **full sun**. The soil should be of **poor to average fertility, neutral to alkaline** and **well drained**. The flowers attract pollinators to the garden.

Tips

These bushy, low growing perennials make a lovely addition to any border.

Recommended

O. majorana (marjoram) is an upright plant with light green, hairy leaves. It bears white or pink flowers in summer and can be grown as an annual where it is not hardy.

O. vulgare var. **hirtum** (oregano, Greek oregano) is the most flavorful culinary variety of oregano. This low-growing, bushy plant has hairy, gray-green leaves and bears white flowers. Many other interesting varieties of *O. vulgare* are available, including those with golden, variegated or curly leaves.

Oregano and marjoram are two of the best-known and most frequently used herbs. They are popular in stuffings, soups and stews, and no pizza is complete until it has been sprinkled with fresh or dried oregano leaves.

In Greek, oros *means 'mountain' and* ganos *means 'joy and beauty,' so oregano translates as 'joy and beauty of the mountain.'*

Features: fragrant foliage; white or pink summer flowers; bushy habit **Height:** 12–32" **Spread:** 8–18" **Hardiness:** zones 5–9

Parsley
Petroselinium

*A*lthough parsley is usually used as a garnish, it is rich in vitamins and minerals and is reputed to freshen the breath after garlic- or onion-rich foods are eaten.

Growing
Parsley grows well in **full sun to partial shade**. The soil should be of **average to rich fertility, humus rich, moist** and **well drained**. Direct sow seeds because the plants resent transplanting. If you start seeds early, use peat pots so the plants can be potted or planted out without disruption.

Tips
Parsley should be started where you mean to grow it as it doesn't transplant well. Containers of parsley can be kept close to the house for easy picking. The bright green leaves and compact growth habit make parsley a good edging plant for beds and borders.

Recommended
P. crispum forms a clump of bright green, divided leaves that stay green all winter. This plant is a biennial but is usually grown as an annual because the leaves are the desired parts, not the flowers or the seeds. Cultivars may have flat or curly leaves. Flat leaves are more flavorful and curly leaves are more decorative. Dwarf cultivars are also available.

P. crispum (above), *P. crispum* var. *crispum* (below)

Parsley leaves make a tasty and nutritious addition to salads. Tear freshly picked leaves and sprinkle them over or mix them in your mixed greens.

Features: attractive foliage **Height:** 8–24"
Spread: 12–24" **Hardiness:** zones 5–8;
grown as an annual or biennial

Rosemary

Rosmarinus

R. officinalis (above & below)

The needle-like leaves of rosemary are used to flavor a wide variety of culinary dishes, including chicken, pork, lamb, rice, tomato, bread and egg dishes.

Growing

Rosemary prefers **full sun** but tolerates partial shade. The soil should be **well drained** and of **poor to average fertility** with a neutral pH. These tender shrubs can be moved indoors for the winter.

Tips

Rosemary is often grown in a shrub border. Low-growing, spreading plants can be included in a rock garden or along the top of a retaining wall, or can be grown in hanging baskets.

Recommended

R. officinalis is a dense, bushy evergreen shrub with narrow, dark green leaves. The habit varies somewhat between cultivars from strongly upright to prostrate and spreading. Prostrate rosemary or *R. officinalis* **'Prostratus'** is not as winter hardy. Flowers are usually in shades of blue, but pink-flowered cultivars are available. Cultivars are available that can survive in zone 6 in a sheltered location with winter protection. The plants rarely reach their mature size when grown in containers.

To overwinter a container-grown plant, keep it in very light or partial shade outdoors in summer, then put it in a sunny window indoors for winter and keep it well watered but allow it to dry out slightly between waterings.

Features: fragrant, evergreen foliage; bright blue, sometimes pink winter flowers
Height: 8"–4' **Spread:** 1–4'
Hardiness: zones 7–10

Sage
Salvia

Sage is perhaps best known as a flavoring for stuffing, but it has a great range of uses and is often included in soups, stews, sausages and dumplings.

Growing
Sage prefers **full sun** but tolerates light shade. The soil should be of **average fertility** and **well drained**. These plants benefit from a light mulch of compost each year. They are drought tolerant once established.

Tips
Sage is an attractive plant for a border, adding volume to the middle, or as an edging or feature plant near the front. Sage can also be grown in mixed planters.

Recommended
S. officinalis is a woody, evergreen, mounding plant with soft, gray-green leaves. Spikes of light purple flowers appear in late spring. Many cultivars with attractive foliage are available, including the silver-leaved **'Berggarten,'** the purple-leaved **'Purpurea,'** the yellow-margined **'Icterina,'** and the purple, green and cream variegated **'Tricolor,'** which has a pink flush to the new growth.

S. *officinalis* 'Icterina' (above)
S. *officinalis* 'Purpurea' (below)

Sage has been used since at least ancient Greek times as a medicinal and culinary herb and continues to be widely used for both these purposes today.

Features: fragrant, decorative foliage; blue or purple flowers **Height:** 12–24"
Spread: 18–36" **Hardiness:** zones 5–8

Sorrel
Rumex

R. acetosa (left), R. scutatus (right)

This may not be one of the most well-known herbs, but it is deserving of wider use. It's not only a lovely dense plant, but its tangy, zesty leaves can be used in soups, salads and many other dishes.

Growing
Sorrel should be grown in **full sun**, but it tolerates partial shade. A **moist, rich, acidic** soil with great **drainage** is best.

The seeds should be sown in late spring. Remove flowerheads when they appear, as the plants can go to seed quite rapidly.

Tips
Sorrel is the perfect addition to any herb or culinary garden for its multiple uses. Sorrel can also adorn ornamental beds when mixed with various perennials, annuals and shrubs.

Do not use sorrel in great quantities or too frequently, as large doses can be poisonous.

Recommended
R. acetosa (common sorrel) is a hardy perennial that produces large, mid-green leaves with a mild flavor. Small flowers are produced but are considered to be inconspicuous.

R. scutatus (French sorrel), the main ingredient in sorrel soup, has smaller leaves that are less bitter, with a hint of lemon.

In locations with excessively warm summers, sorrel leaves can become bitter as the season progresses. Mulching around the base of the plants helps to keep the soil cooler and improves the flavor of the leaves.

Features: dense growth habit; ornamental and useful foliage **Height:** 2–4'
Spread: 12–24" **Hardiness:** zones 4–8

Sweet Basil

Ocimum

The sweet, fragrant leaves of fresh basil add a delicious, licorice-like flavor to salads, pesto and tomato-based dishes.

Growing

Sweet basil grows best in a **warm, sheltered** location in **full sun**. The soil should be **fertile, moist** and **well drained**. Pinch the tips regularly to encourage bushy growth. Plant out or direct sow seed after frost danger has passed in spring.

Tips

Although sweet basil will grow best in a warm spot outdoors, it can be grown successfully indoors in a pot by a bright window to provide you with fresh leaves all year.

Recommended

O. basilicum is one of the most popular of the culinary herbs. There are dozens of varieties, including ones with large or tiny, green or purple and smooth or ruffled leaves. *O. tenuiflorum* (syn. *O. sanctum*, sacred basil, holy basil) is an aromatic annual or short-lived perennial with an upright habit and grayish green leaves. The flavor is reminiscent of cloves and complements salads and other cold dishes.

O. basilicum 'Genovese' (above & below)

Sweet basil is a good companion plant for tomatoes—both like warm, moist growing conditions and when you pick tomatoes for a salad you'll also remember to include a few sprigs or leaves of basil.

Features: fragrant, decorative leaves
Height: 12–24" **Spread:** 12–18"
Hardiness: tender annual

Thyme
Thymus

T. vulgaris (above), T. x citriodorus (below)

Thyme is a popular culinary herb used when cooking soups, stews, casseroles and roasts.

Growing

Thyme prefers **full sun**. The soil should be **neutral to alkaline** and of **poor to average fertility**. **Good drainage** is essential.

It is beneficial to work leaf mold and sharp limestone gravel into the soil to improve structure and drainage.

Tips

Thyme is useful for sunny, dry locations at the front of borders, between or beside paving stones, on rock gardens and rock walls and in containers.

Once the plants have finished flowering, shear them back by about half to encourage new growth and to prevent the plants from becoming too woody.

Recommended

T. x *citriodorus* (lemon-scented thyme) forms a mound of lemon-scented, dark green foliage. The flowers are pale pink. Cultivars with silver- or gold-margined leaves are available.

T. vulgaris (common thyme) forms a bushy mound of dark green leaves. The flowers may be purple, pink or white. Cultivars with variegated leaves are available.

These plants are bee magnets when blooming; thyme honey is pleasantly herbal and goes very well with biscuits.

Features: bushy habit; fragrant, decorative foliage; purple, pink, white flowers **Height:** 8–16" **Spread:** 8–16" **Hardiness:** zones 4–9

Angel's Trumpet

Datura/Brugmansia

*A*ngel's trumpets add an exotic accent to the garden with their elegant, funnel-shaped, fragrant flowers.

Growing

Angel's trumpets prefer **full sun**. The soil should be **fertile, moist** and **well drained**. Water these plants sparingly, just enough to keep the soil from drying out but don't allow them to completely dry out, particularly during hot weather. Plants recover quickly from wilting when watered.

Tips

Angel's trumpet flowers tend to open at night. Grow these plants where you can enjoy their intoxicating scent in the evening near a patio or in a large container on a deck. They are attractive as specimens or in groups.

Recommended

These plants are divided into two different, but closely related, genera. In general, herbaceous annuals and perennials with upward-facing flowers are classified as *Datura,* whereas the woody plants with pendulous flowers are classified as *Brugmansia.* This rule of thumb is only slightly helpful because many of the woody plants are treated as tender annuals or perennials and are discarded before they become woody. Many catalogs and garden

D. metel (above), *D. innoxia* (below)

centers name the plants incorrectly, and even the scientific names of the various species are in a state of confusion. So, find the plant you like and don't worry too much about its name.

Many species, hybrids and cultivars are available in various forms, sizes and flower colors, including white, purple, apricot, yellow, pink, orange or cream. The flowers are sometimes single but can also be double.

All parts of this plant are poisonous if ingested.

Features: fragrant, large flowers; soft foliage and form **Height:** 5–15' **Spread:** 5–15'
Hardiness: grown as an annual

Autumn Fern

Dryopteris

D. erythrosora (above & below)

This is a lovely, easy-to-grow fern that offers color, interest and a touch of class to any shady location.

Growing

Autumn fern grows best in **partial shade** but tolerates more sun in damp soil. The soil should be **fertile, humus rich** and **moist** but autumn fern will acclimate to less-than-ideal locations. Divide the plant to control spread and to propagate.

The common name refers to the fact that younger fronds look like they have been brushed with copper when the weather gets cooler in fall.

Tips

Autumn fern is an impressive evergreen fern that is useful in a shaded area or a woodland garden. It is an ideal fern to include in an area of the garden that stays moist or periodically floods.

Recommended

D. erythrosora produces 18–24" long, arching fronds and spreads by short, creeping rhizomes. This fern is distinguished by its young, bronze, glossy foliage that matures to a deep, dark green. It is very upright in form and the foliage is supported by dark stems.

Features: decorative fronds; upright growth habit **Height:** 24" **Spread:** 12–24" **Hardiness:** zones 5–9

Cast Iron Plant

Aspidistra

*T*he name cast iron plant wasn't given in vain, as this perennial prefers to grow in deep shade conditions where little else roams.

Growing

Cast iron plant prefers to grow in **partial or full shade**. Bright, direct sunlight and winter winds will burn its leaves. Cast iron plant is drought tolerant, but **well-drained, organically rich** soil is a benefit.

Tips

This perennial is perfect in deeply shaded areas, including that gap under your deck that's visible from the rest of the garden and where little else will grow. It is useful in woodland settings, shaded borders and in tight, sheltered areas between houses where the sun cannot get to.

Recommended

A. elatior produces upright, large, arching leaves with distinctive textural veining from stem to tip. The leaves can reach 1–3' lengths with 4–6" widths. Inconspicuous flowers are borne in spring. Additional selections are available with white variegations of differing patterns.

A. elatior (above & below)

Cast iron plant is well suited to growing in decorative containers. It can be placed in locations that require a vertical element in formal to casual settings, where a lack of sunlight prevails.

Features: shade tolerance; form **Height:** 3–4'
Spread: 3–4' **Hardiness:** zones 7–10

Christmas Fern

Polystichum

P. acrostitchoides (above & below)

These native, evergreen ferns are a treat, providing greenery all year, not just during the Christmas season.

Growing

Christmas fern grows well in **partial, light or full shade**. The soil should be **fertile, humus rich** and **moist** but this fern also survives in dry shade. Remove dead and withered fronds in spring before the new ones fill in.

Christmas fern is hardy and low growing and is less invasive than many of its fern cousins. It is native to eastern North America.

Tips

Christmas fern makes an attractive addition to shaded beds and borders and can be included in a woodland garden. If you have a pond, these ferns can be used in moist, shaded areas near it.

Recommended

P. acrostichoides forms circular clusters of evergreen fronds. The fronds also display an arching habit. This species spreads with underground rhizomes and often has multiple crowns. Many cultivars are available with ruffled, crested or deeply toothed fronds.

This plant received its common name because it is visible at Christmas time and was used by early settlers for holiday decorations.

Features: lush, ornate, evergreen foliage
Height: 12–24" **Spread:** 12–36"
Hardiness: zones 3–9

Cinnamon Fern
Osmunda

$\mathcal{F}$erns have a certain prehistoric mystique and can add a graceful elegance and textural accent to the garden.

Growing

Flowering ferns prefer **light shade** but tolerate part sun if the soil is consistently moist. The soil should be **fertile, humus rich, acidic** and **moist**. Flowering ferns tolerate wet soil and will spread as offsets form at the plant bases.

Tips

These large ferns form an attractive mass when planted in large colonies. They can be included in beds and borders and make a welcome addition to a woodland garden.

Recommended

O. cinnamomea (cinnamon fern) has light green, 2½–5' long fronds that fan out in a circular fashion from a central point.

O. regalis (above), *O. cinnamomea* (below)

Bright green, leafless, fertile fronds that mature to cinnamon brown are produced in spring and stand straight up in the center of the plant. This deciduous fern is cold tolerant and does best from the piedmont to the mountains.

O. regalis (royal fern, flowering fern) forms a dense clump of foliage. Feathery, flower-like, fertile fronds stand out among the sterile fronds in summer and mature to a rusty brown.

This species grows equally as tall and in similar form to the other species. **'Purpurescens'** fronds are purple-red when they emerge in spring, and mature to green. This contrasts well with its purple stems. (Zones 3–8)

The flowering fern's 'flowers' are actually its spore-producing sporangia.

Features: deciduous, perennial fern; decorative, fertile fronds; habit **Height:** 2–5' **Spread:** 2–5' **Hardiness:** zones 2–8

Common Maidenhair Fern
Adiantum

A. pedatum (above & below)

These charming and delicate-looking native ferns add a graceful touch to any woodland planting. Their unique habit and texture will stand out in any garden.

Growing
Common maidenhair fern grows well in **light to partial shade** but tolerates full shade. The soil should be of **average fertility, humus rich, slightly acidic** and **moist**. Allow plenty of room for good air circulation.

This plant rarely needs dividing, but it can be divided in spring to propagate more plants.

Tips
These lovely ferns do well in any shaded spot. Include them in rock gardens, woodland gardens, shaded borders and beneath shade trees. They also make an attractive addition to a shaded planting next to a water feature, or on a slope where the foliage can be seen when it sways in the breeze.

Recommended
A. capillus-veneris (Southern maidenhair fern) is a great fern for the warmer areas of the Carolinas. It produces light green, lacy foliage on triangular fronds with thin, black stems. This species grows 1' tall and wide.

A. pedatum (Northern maidenhair fern) forms a spreading mound of delicate, arching fronds arranged in a horseshoe or circular pattern. This species is tolerant to colder temperatures in zones 3–8. Its light green leaflets stand out against the black stems, and the whole plant turns bright yellow in fall. Spores are produced on the undersides of the leaflets.

Features: deciduous, perennial fern; summer and fall foliage; habit **Height:** 12–30"
Spread: 12–24" **Hardiness:** zones 3–10

Epimedium
Epimedium

*L*ong lived and low maintenance with attractive, heart-
shaped, often-colorful foliage and
delicate sprays of tiny, orchid-like
flowers, this plant is a woodland
garden favorite.

Growing
Epimedium grows best in **light
shade** or **partial shade** but tolerates full shade. The soil should be
average to fertile, humus rich
and **moist**, though the plants are
fairly drought tolerant once
established. Cut back the foliage,
especially if it looks tattered,
before new growth begins in late
winter.

Tips
These winter- to spring-blooming
plants are a popular addition to
shade and woodland gardens, as
accent plants or groundcovers.
They can be planted under taller,
shade-providing plants in beds
and borders as well as in moist,
pondside plantings. Epimedium
can be slow to establish, but it's
worth the wait.

Recommended
There are many available species
hybrids and cultivars grown for
their attractive foliage and spring
flowers. Plants may be clump forming or spreading in habit. *E.* x
cantabrigiense is a clump-forming
plant with dark green leaves and
coppery orange flowers touched

E. x *rubrum* (above & below)

with red. *E. grandiflorum* is also a
clump-forming plant. Its cultivars have creamy white
to dark pink flowers.
E. x *perralchium*
'Frohnleiten' is a
compact, spread-
ing plant with
bright yellow
flowers and
reddish green
foliage that persists into winter.
E. x *rubrum*, a low-spreading
plant with small, wine- and
cream-colored flowers, is
one of the most popular
groundcover selections.

Also called: bishop's hat **Features:** yellow,
orange, cream, white, pink, red, purple spring
flowers; foliage; habit **Height:** 6–18"
Spread: 12–24" **Hardiness:** zones 4–8

Feather Reed Grass

Calamagrostis

C. x *acutiflora* 'Overdam' (above)
C. x *acutiflora* 'Karl Foerster' (below)

This is a graceful, metamorphic grass that changes its habit and flower color throughout the seasons. The slightest breeze keeps this grass in perpetual motion.

Growing

Feather reed grass grows best in **full sun**. The soil should be **fertile, moist** and **well drained**. Heavy clay and dry soils are tolerated. It may be susceptible to rust in cool, wet summers or in sites with poor air circulation.

Rain and heavy snow may cause reed grass to flop temporarily, but it quickly bounces back.

Cut back the plant to 2–4" in very early spring before growth begins. Divide reed grass if it begins to die out in the center.

Tips

Whether used as a single, stately focal point in small groupings or in large drifts, this grass is a desirable, low-maintenance grass. It combines well with late-summer and fall-blooming perennials.

Recommended

C. x *acutiflora* 'Karl Foerster' (Foerster's feather reed grass), the most popular selection, forms a loose mound of green foliage from which the airy, distinctly vertical, bottlebrush flowers emerge in late spring. The flowering stems have a loose, arching habit when they first emerge but grow more stiff and upright over summer. Other cultivars include **'Overdam,'** a compact, less heat-tolerant selection with white leaf edges. Watch for a new introduction called **'Avalanche,'** which has a white center stripe.

Features: open habit; green foliage turns bright gold in fall; winter interest; silvery pink and tan flowerheads **Height:** 3–5'
Spread: 24–36" **Hardiness:** zones 4–9

Green and Gold

Chrysogonum

This native perennial groundcover is found growing at the woodland's edge from southern Pennsylvania to Florida. This is a great indication of its preference to southern climates and soils. Green and gold is sure to impress with its bright yellow blossoms that resemble mini-sunflowers or zinnias.

Growing

Green and gold prefers **partial to full shade**. Any soil type is fine if very **well drained**. Adding humus isn't necessary, but it can be an added benefit.

Tips

This spreading perennial is often used as a flowering groundcover, as it spreads by way of underground rhizomes. It can also be used at the front of perennial and shrub borders for a blast of bright color from early spring and off and on through late fall.

Recommended

C. virginianum (green and gold) forms an attractive mat of toothed, coarsely textured foliage. Bright yellow, starry-shaped blossoms emerge in early spring and continue to bloom sporadically until fall. A few cultivars are available with dark green leaves, wider spreads, longer blooming periods and more vigorous growth habits.

C. virginianum (above & below)

Chrysogonum *comes from the Greek word* chrusos, *which means 'golden,' and* gonu *which translates to 'knee.'*

Features: bright yellow flowers; lush foliage; habit **Height:** 8–10" **Spread:** 18–24"
Hardiness: zones 5–8

Holly Fern

Arachniodes

A. simplicior (above & below)

Each fern has at least one unique characteristic. The delicate fronds of the variegated *Arachniodes* selection are lined with yellow, distinguishing them from all others. What else might you discover?

Growing

Shady locations in **organically, humus-rich** soil that is **moist** but **well drained** are best.

Tips

Woodland settings and shady borders are often the best place to plant ferns of any type. Holly fern is the perfect complement to bolder leaved plants and low-growing groundcovers with variegation in their leaves.

Recommended

A. simplicior forms an erect clump of deeply cut, shiny foliage that is dark green in color. This species is considered to be evergreen in the lower and coastal portions of the state but semi-evergreen towards the mountains. **'Variegata'** produces shiny, dark fronds with a yellow stripe down the center of each segment.

Features: delicate, finely cut, dark green fronds; habit **Height:** 10–18"
Spread: 24–36" **Hardiness:** zones 6–9

Japanese Forest Grass

Hakonechloa

*J*apanese forest grass is an attractive, shade-loving grass that provides interest throughout the growing season.

Growing

Japanese forest grass prefers **light** or **partial shade** but tolerates part sun if the soil is kept moist. The soil should be **fertile, rich in organic matter, moist** and **well drained**. Use an organic mulch to maintain soil moisture as these plants resent drying out. If the foliage becomes scorched, move the plant to a more shaded location. Mulch well in winter to protect the plants.

Tips

Japanese forest grass is one of the few grass plants that grows well in shaded locations. Its texture and color is a good contrast to broad-leaved shade plants. This grass makes an attractive addition to mixed beds and borders and can be used along the tops of retaining walls where its arching habit will show well. It is also striking spilling over the side of containers.

Recommended

H. macra has bright green, arching, grass-like foliage. The foliage turns deep pink in fall, then bronze as winter sets in. Several cultivars are available. **'Albo-Striata'** has green-and-white-striped leaves. **'All Gold'**

H. macra 'Aureola' (above & below)

has pure gold leaves and is more upright and spiky in habit. **'Aureola'** has bright yellow foliage with narrow, green streaks; the foliage turns pink in fall. Yellow-leaved cultivars may scorch in full sun and lose their yellow color in too much shade.

This ornamental grass is native to Japan, where it grows on mountainsides and cliffsides, often near streams and other water sources.

Features: arching habit; fall color
Height: 12–24" **Spread:** 12–24"
Hardiness: zones 5–9

Japanese Painted Fern
Athyrium

A. niponicum var. *pictum* 'Silver Falls' (above)
A. felix-femina (below)

Japanese painted ferns are some of the most well-behaved ferns, adding color and texture to shady spots without growing out of control.

Growing
Both fern species grow well in **full shade, partial shade** or **light shade**. The soil should be of **average fertility, humus rich, acidic** and **moist**. Division is rarely required but can be done to propagate more plants.

Tips
Lady and Japanese painted ferns form an attractive mass of foliage, but they don't grow out of control like some ferns tend to. Include them in shade gardens and moist woodland gardens.

Recommended
A. filix-femina (lady fern) forms a dense clump of lacy fronds. It grows 12–24" tall and has a 24" spread. Cultivars are available, including dwarf cultivars and cultivars with variable foliage. Var. *asplenioides* (Southern lady fern) is a native form with more triangular fronds.

A. niponicum var. *pictum* '**Metallicum**' (Japanese painted fern) forms a clump of dark green fronds with a silvery or reddish metallic sheen. It grows 12–24" tall and has a 24" spread. Many cultivars of *A. niponicum* var. *pictum* are available. Some of the more colorful cultivars include '**Burgundy Lace,**' with metallic burgundy leaves; '**Pewter Lace,**' with fine, metallic gray foliage; and '**Ursula's Red,**' with iridescent, silver-white and rich maroon-red leaves. (Zones 4–8)

The colorful foliage of the Japanese painted fern will brighten up any shaded area with its metallic shades of silver, burgundy and bronze.

Features: habit; foliage **Height:** 12–24"
Spread: 12–24" **Hardiness:** zones 3–8

Juncus

Juncus

Juncus is a foliar specimen but it's often mistaken for a grass. The stems are hollow and cylindrical rather than flat and broad. This unique plant is a must for any type of water-related garden.

Growing
Juncus grows best in **sun** or **partial shade**. The soil should be **consistently moist, if not wet**, and **slightly acidic**. It can be grown in a small container or submerged in water up to the crown in a water feature or pond.

Tips
Juncus is considered a marginal perennial. It is well suited to bog gardens, locations that remain moist for long periods and water gardens.

Recommended
J. effusus (juncus, rush) is a tender perennial, wetland plant that grows in a clump and spreads by vigorous underground rhizomes. Erect clumps of slightly arching, cylindrical stems can grow up to 36". **'Cuckoo'** has longitudinal yellow stripes, whereas **'Spiralis'** (spiral rush or corkscrew rush) is a low-growing rush with curly, spiraling stems. **'Unicorn'** is an exaggerated version of 'Spiralis,' producing thicker, longer, curled stems; **'Vittatus'** has narrow, creamy white bands; and **'Zebrinus'** has broad white bands.

J. effusus 'Cuckoo' (above), *J. effusus* 'Spiralis' (below)

J. inflexus (hard rush) is an upright rush, with bluish gray stems that form a 24–30" tall and wide clump. **'Afro'** is a little shorter than the species but grows just as wide, bearing coiled stems.

Juncus can overwinter outdoors if buried in a well-protected, moist area and covered with several inches of bark mulch or leaf matter. It can also be brought indoors and treated as a houseplant until its return outdoors in spring.

Features: foliage; form; versatility
Height: 18–36" **Spread:** 12–36"
Hardiness: zones 4–8

Mondo Grass

Ophiopogon

O. japonicus 'Gyoko Ryu' (above)
O. japonicus 'Bluebird' (below)

Tips

Mondo grass can be used as a dense groundcover and for erosion control as it spreads by rhizomes. Use it for border edges and containers.

Recommended

O. japonicus (mondo grass, monkey grass) produces dark green, grass-like foliage that grows 8–14" long and forms an evergreen mat of lush foliage, resembling an unkempt lawn. Short spikes of white, occasionally lilac-tinged flowers emerge in summer, followed by metallic blue fruit. Many cultivars are available in dwarf forms and variegated forms.

O. planiscapus 'Ebknizam' EBONY NIGHT (black mondo grass, black lily turf) has curving, almost black leaves and dark lavender flowers. It grows 4–6" tall and 6–12" wide. 'Nigrescens' has curving, almost black foliage and pink to white-flushed pink flowers. It grows 6–12" tall and 12" wide. Both cultivars produce blackish, berry-like fruit.

Mondo grass is an excellent groundcover, accent and contrast plant. The foliage displayed by black mondo grass is the perfect dark background to highlight any brightly colored plant or flower.

Growing

Mondo grass prefers to grow in **partial sun to light shade** in **moist, moderately fertile, well-drained, humus-rich** soil. The foliage is at its best in part sun. Divide in spring just as new growth resumes. These plants appreciate some winter protection of thick mulch in zones 5 and 6, but are otherwise left uncovered.

This plant is a member of the same family as lilies and does not like being mowed.

Features: uniquely colored foliage; groundcover habit; lavender, pink, white-flushed pink flowers **Height:** 4–12" **Spread:** 6–12" **Hardiness:** zones 5–9

Muhly Grass
Muhlenbergia

*Y*ou may think you're witnessing some kind of unusual atmospheric phenomenon, when in fact it's the pinkish purple haze of the flower plumes borne from muhly grass. It's bound to leave you wanting more.

Growing

Muhly grass thrives in bright, **sunny** locations in **well-drained, moist** soil. Light shade is tolerated. Once established, muhly grass prefers dryer soil that is well aerated; however, it is tolerant to just about any soil type.

Muhly grass is known to self-seed. If you want thicker stands, leave the ripened seedheads in place, allowing the ripened seed to fall, which results in a thicker, larger and more dense clump of grass. Otherwise, remove the seedheads before they ripen and fall.

Tips

This wild-looking, medium-sized grass is suited to mixed beds and borders with bolder-leaved plants, bringing attention to its delicate appeal. It's also useful for naturalizing areas of your garden that require little attention or care and works well as a groundcover in areas with poor soil. The fall color stands out while most other plants look spent.

M. capillaris (above & below)

Recommended

M. capillaris (syn. *M. filipes;* gulf muhlygrass, mist grass, hairy awn muhly, pink muhlygrass, purple muhlygrass) produces a knee-high, dense stand of fine, wispy grass that is grayish green. This showy clump can reach 3–4' heights and spreads. Purplish flowerheads emerge in late summer and last for up to two months. **'Regal Mist'** bears rosy pink flowers. **'White Cloud'** has white flowers.

Features: form; purple seedheads in fall
Height: 3–4' **Spread:** 3–4'
Hardiness: zones 5–10

Pachysandra
Pachysandra

P. terminalis (above & below)

Low-maintenance pachysandra is one of the most popular ground-covers. Its rhizomatous rootzone colonizes quickly to form a dense blanket over the ground.

Growing
Pachysandra prefers **light to full shade** but tolerates partial shade. Any soil that is **moist, acidic, humus rich** and **well drained** is good. Plants can be propagated easily from cuttings or by division.

Tips
Pachysandras are durable groundcovers under trees, in shady borders and in woodland gardens. The foliage is considered evergreen but winter-scorched shoots may need to be removed in spring.

Interplant this popular groundcover with spring bulbs, hostas or ferns, or use it as an underplanting for deciduous trees and shrubs with contrasting foliage colors.

Recommended
P. procumbens (Allegheny spurge) is a native evergreen, low-growing species that bears white flowers. Its leaves are interestingly mottled. This species is not aggressive and grows 6–12" tall. It is sadly underused.

P. terminalis (Japanese spurge) forms a low mass of evergreen foliage rosettes. It grows about 8" tall and can spread almost indefinitely. '**Variegata**' has white margins or mottled silver foliage, but it is not as vigorous as the species. '**Green Sheen**' has, as its name implies, exceptionally glossy leaves that are smaller than those of the species.

Features: perennial, evergreen groundcover; habit; inconspicuous, fragrant, white, spring flowers **Height:** 6–12" **Spread:** 12–18" or more **Hardiness:** zones 3–8

Pitcher Plants

Sarracenia

Pitcher plants are a fascinating group of native insectivores. They're fun to grow and are an unusual addition to just about any setting.

Growing

Pitcher plants prefer locations with **full to partial sun**. The soil should be consistently **moist to boggy** and **acidic**. Pitcher plants thrive in nutrient-depleted soils, so fertilizing isn't necessary; they absorb the necessary nutrients from the insects they consume.

Tips

Pitcher plants are ideal for locations that are kept consistently moist but not flooded. Bog gardens are the best-suited location as long as the area receives full to partial sun.

Recommended

S. flava (yellow pitcher plant) produces erect, pitcher-shaped foliage in yellowish green with crimson veining. It bears bright yellow, pendulous flowers that stand tall, often taller than the pitchers. The species grows 24–36" tall and wide.

S. **hybrids** are a group of many complex selections that are available in a wide array of forms, colors and sizes. They are vigorous growers, painted with color beyond your wildest imagination. Ask your local garden center for their recommendations.

S. hybrid (above), S. flava (below)

S. minor (hooded pitcher plant) is a smaller, native plant that only grows to 1' tall. It produces green and coppery red, pitcher-like foliage with domed lids or hoods and yellowish green flowers in late spring.

S. purpurea (parrot pitcher plant) produces jug-shaped pitchers up to 12" long that lie along the ground. The colors range from green with red veining to burgundy and red. Purple, red, pink or purplish red flowers are borne in spring.

Features: pendent, colorful flowers; interesting pitcher-like foliage **Height:** 12–36"
Spread: 12–24" **Hardiness:** zones 5–10

Sedge
Carex

C. comans 'Frosted Curls' (above)

'Sedges have edges,' the opening line to a classic gardener's poem, points out that sedges, unlike true grasses, have triangular stems. Sedge foliage comes in green, blue, rust, bronze or gold, which allows the gardener to add broad, colorful strokes to the landscape.

Growing
Most sedges grow well in **full sun to partial shade** in **moist, well-drained, neutral to slightly alkaline** soil. 'Frosted Curls' prefers average to dry soil and is drought tolerant once established. Propagate by seed or division of clumps in mid-spring to early summer.

Tips
Use these plants in rock gardens, water features, containers and borders. The fine foliage of 'Frosted Curls' contrasts well with coarse-textured plants.

Stems can be cut to the ground in early spring before new growth occurs, or they can be 'combed' to remove the older foliage.

Recommended
There are many sedges available. *C. buchananii* (leatherleaf sedge) is a densely tufted, evergreen perennial with an arching habit and orange-brown foliage; *C. comans* **'Frosted Curls'** (*C.* 'Frosted Curls'; New Zealand hair sedge) is a compact, clump-forming, evergreen perennial with fine-textured, very pale green, weeping foliage. The foliage appears almost iridescent, with unusual curled and twisted tips; *C. grayi* (Gray's sedge) has star-like seedheads and clumps of rich green leaves; *C. plantaginea* (seersucker sedge) has bright green leaves with many veins and showy flowers; *C. siderosticha* **'Variegata'** (striped broad-leaved sedge) resembles a mass of narrow, 1" wide hosta leaves.

Features: interesting, colorful foliage; growth habit **Height:** 6–36" **Spread:** 24–36" **Hardiness:** zones 5–9

Sedum

Sedum

Some 300 to 500 species of sedum are distributed throughout the Northern Hemisphere. Sedums are generally grown for their foliage, which ranges in color from steel gray-blue and green to red and burgundy. Their broccoli-like flowers bloom in late summer to fall, then turn brown and persist through winter.

Growing

Sedums prefer **full sun** but tolerate partial shade. The soil should be of **average fertility, very well drained** and **neutral**. Divide in spring when needed.

Tips

Low-growing sedums make wonderful groundcovers and additions to rock gardens or rock walls. They edge beds and borders beautifully. Taller sedums give a lovely late-season display in a bed or border.

Recommended

Many species, hybrids and cultivars are available. Listed below are some of the more popular selections.

S. **'Autumn Joy'** (*S.* 'Herbstfreude'; autumn joy sedum) is a popular, upright hybrid. The flowers open pink or red and fade to deep bronze.

S. **'Frosty Morn'** resembles 'Autumn Joy' but the leaves are edged in white with pale pink flowers in fall.

S. 'Autumn Joy' (above & below)

S. **'Purple Emperor'** (purple autumn stonecrop) is an upright plant with wine red to purple foliage and dusty pink flowers.

S. x **'Vera Jameson'** is a low-growing, spreading selection with bronze foliage and purple-pink flowers.

S. *spurium* (two-row stonecrop) is a popular, mat-forming evergreen with deep pink or white flowers. Cultivars are available and are often grown for their colorful foliage, including **'John Creech.'**

Features: yellow, white, red, pink, green summer to autumn flowers; decorative, fleshy foliage **Height:** 2–24" **Spread:** 12–24" or more **Hardiness:** zones 3–8

Solomon's Seal

Polygonatum

Solomon's seal is a native woodland wildflower with graceful, arching stems that add a horizontal element to an understory planting.

Growing

Solomon's seal prefers **partial to full shade**. Direct afternoon sun can harm or burn this plant. The soil should be **fertile, humus rich, moist** and **well drained**.

Tips

Solomon's seal seems to brighten up the darkest shade garden. It works well in mixed beds and borders but looks most at home in woodland settings or naturalized areas. It is suitable as a groundcover when mass planted. The berries are highly **poisonous**.

Recommended

P. biflorum (small Solomon's seal) is a native perennial with arching stems bearing narrow leaves and pendent, tubular, greenish white flowers that dangle just under the stems and leaves. The species grows 1–3' tall and 2' wide.

P. falcatum **Silver Stripe Form** (silver stripe Solomon's seal) is a new, 2' tall selection with a silver stripe down the center of each leaf. Small, pendent, white flowers dangle beneath the stems in early spring.

P. odoratum (fragrant Solomon's seal) grows 24" tall and 12–24" wide. It has arching stems and spreads slowly by rhizomes. Pendent, green-tipped, white flowers are borne along the stem in spring to early summer. Black, round berries follow the waxy flowers. **'Variegatum'** has white-edged variegated foliage. New stems are red.

Features: foliage; white flowers; habit
Height: 24–36" **Spread:** 12–30"
Hardiness: zones 4–8

Strawberry Begonia

Saxifraga

S. *stolonifera* 'Kinki Purple' (above), S. *stolonifera* (below)

There are more than 400 species of *Saxifraga* and even more cultivars, but the strawberry begonia or S. *stolonifera* is probably one of the best selections for the Carolinas for all it has to offer and its tolerance to excessive heat.

Growing

Strawberry begonia prefers to be planted in **partial to full shade**. The soil should be **neutral to alkaline, fertile, moist** and **well drained**, but it has been known to grow just about anywhere. Divide in spring.

Tips

Strawberry begonia is an excellent addition to rock gardens and borders and works well in shaded mixed borders. It can also be used as a groundcover in moist soil.

Features: white summer flowers; attractive foliage; spreading habit **Height:** 12–24" **Spread:** 24" **Hardiness:** zones 7–9

Recommended

S. *stolonifera* (strawberry begonia, strawberry geranium, mother of thousands) produces a thick, semi-evergreen mat of attractively gray-veined leaves with purple undersides and tiny white flowers borne on spikes. The parent plant sends out shoots at the end of which grow tiny new plants. **'Harvest Moon'** produces golden foliage and pink flowers, and **'Tricolor'** has rich green, cupped leaves edged in white and pink with deeper pink underneath, and white flowers.

This perennial groundcover is neither a begonia nor a geranium but displays physical characteristics reminiscent of both. Strawberry begonia is a beautiful addition to hanging baskets.

Sweet Flag
Acorus

A. calamus 'Variegatus' (above)
A. gramineus cultivar (below)

These grass-like plants are most at home in wet and boggy locations, making them a favorite of water gardeners.

Growing

Sweet flag grows best in **partial sun to shade**. The soil should be **fertile** and **moist** or **wet**. Divide plants to propagate and to prevent clumps from becoming too dense.

Tips

These plants are much admired for their habit as well as for the wonderful, spicy fragrance of the crushed leaves. Include sweet flag in moist borders or at the margins of your pond if you have one. They can also be grown in containers.

Recommended

A. calamus (sweet flag) is a large, clump-forming plant with long, narrow, bright green, fragrant foliage. It grows 2–5' tall with about a 24" spread. **'Variegatus'** is a popular and commonly available cultivar that has yellow, cream and green vertically striped leaves.

A. gramineus (Japanese rush, dwarf sweet flag) is a smaller, clump-forming plant with glossy, green, fragrant leaves. It grows 4–12" tall with an equal spread. The cultivar **'Ogon'** is prized for its bright, golden, variegated foliage. (Zones 5–8)

Sweet flag was a popular moat-side plant in the past, and the fragrant leaves were spread on floors to keep rooms smelling sweet.

Features: attractive habit and foliage
Height: 4"–5' **Spread:** 4–24"
Hardiness: zones 4–8

Venus Flytrap
Dionaea

Insects are no match for this insectivorous perennial, and kids of all ages are sure to love its carnivorous ways.

Growing

Venus flytrap prefers to grow in **full to partial sun**. This is only possible if it is grown in soil that is kept consistently **moist to wet**. **Acidic** soil is also preferred. Plants go semi-dormant in winter. Venus flytrap should not be fertilized.

To encourage new growth, but more specifically new traps, pinch out newly emerging flower stems and spent blackened traps.

D. muscipula (above & below)

Tips

This native perennial is found where bogs are prevalent near Wilmington, North Carolina. It's important to replicate its native habitat by choosing a location that is exposed to sunlight but remains moist, like a bog garden. Venus flytrap plants remain tiny and need to be planted where they won't be lost.

Recommended

D. muscipula is a rosette-forming perennial bearing semi-evergreen, rounded, chartreuse to red leaves with winged stems. The leaves can reach 5–6" lengths. At the end of each stem are two hinged lobes lined with bristle-like glands. The glands produce nectar that insects are attracted to. Small, sensitive hairs inside the trap let the plant know that an insect has landed, signaling the lobes to come together to capture the insect. This allows the plant to obtain nutrients that are unavailable in the soil. A couple of cultivars are available with bright red coloration on both the stems and traps.

Features: fascinating form and habit
Height: 6–18" **Spread:** 6–8"
Hardiness: zones 8–10

Wild Ginger

Asarum

A. canadense (above), A. europaeum (below)

Ginger is a beautiful groundcover for woodland sites. Glossy, heart-shaped leaves form a low-growing mat that grows quickly but is not invasive.

Growing

Wild ginger needs **full or partial shade**. The soil should be **moist** and **humus rich**. All *Asarum* species prefer **acidic** soils, but *A. canadense* tolerates alkaline conditions. Ginger can tolerate dry conditions for a while in good shade, but prolonged drought causes wilt and dieback.

Tips

Use ginger in a shady rock garden, border or woodland garden. Ginger is relatively easy to remove from places where it isn't welcome.

Recommended

A. arifolium (arrow-leaf ginger) is a native evergreen, with 8–10" wide leaves, marked with a distinctive triangle shape and mottled coloration.

A. canadense (Canada wild ginger) has slightly hairy, heart-shaped deciduous leaves. The roots of this wild ginger can be used in place of true ginger (*Zinciber officinale*) in recipes.

A. europaeum (European wild ginger) forms an expanding clump of very glossy evergreen leaves, often distinctively silver-veined. This species is not as heat tolerant as *A. canadense.*

A. shuttleworthii (Shuttleworth ginger) is an evergreen native with rounded, mottled foliage. 'Callaway' has mottled foliage, and 'Eco Medallion' produces silvery foliage with a compact habit.

Features: burgundy or green, inconspicuous flowers; sometimes grown for attractive foliage; easy to grow **Height:** 3–6" **Spread:** 12" **Hardiness:** zones 4–8

Glossary

Acid soil: soil with a pH lower than 7.0

Annual: a plant that germinates, flowers, sets seed and dies in one growing season

Alkaline soil: soil with a pH higher than 7.0

Basal leaves: leaves that form from the crown, at the base of the plant

Bract: a modified leaf at the base of a flower or flower cluster

Corm: a bulb-like, food-storing, underground stem, resembling a bulb without scales

Crown: the part of the plant at or just below soil level where the shoots join the roots

Cultivar: a cultivated plant variety with one or more distinct differences from the species, e.g., in flower color or disease resistance

Damping off: fungal disease causing seedlings to rot at soil level and topple over

Deadhead: to remove spent flowers to maintain a neat appearance and encourage a longer blooming season

Direct sow: to sow seeds directly in the garden

Dormancy: a period of plant inactivity, usually during winter or unfavorable conditions

Double flower: a flower with an unusually large number of petals

Genus: a category of biological classification between the species and family levels; the first word in a scientific name indicates the genus

Grafting: a type of propagation in which a stem or bud of one plant is joined onto the rootstock of another plant of a closely related species

Hardy: capable of surviving unfavorable conditions, such as cold weather or frost, without protection

Hip: the fruit of a rose, containing the seeds

Humus: decomposed or decomposing organic material in the soil

Hybrid: a plant resulting from natural or human-induced cross-breeding between varieties, species or genera

Inflorescence: a flower cluster

Male clone: a plant that may or may not produce pollen but that will not produce fruit, seed or seedpods

Neutral soil: soil with a pH of 7.0

Perennial: a plant that takes three or more years to complete its life cycle

pH: a measure of acidity or alkalinity; the soil pH influences availability of nutrients for plants

Rhizome: a root-like, food-storing stem that grows horizontally at or just below soil level, from which new shoots may emerge

Rootball: the root mass and surrounding soil of a plant

Seedhead: dried, inedible fruit that contains seeds; the fruiting stage of the inflorescence

Self-seeding: reproducing by means of seeds without human assistance, so that new plants constantly replace those that die

Semi-double flower: a flower with petals in two or three rings

Single flower: a flower with a single ring of typically four or five petals

Species: the fundamental unit of biological classification; the entity from which cultivars and varieties are derived

Standard: a shrub or small tree grown with an erect main stem, accomplished either through pruning and training or by grafting the plant onto a tall, straight stock

Sucker: a shoot that comes up from the root, often some distance from the plant; it can be separated to form a new plant once it develops its own roots

Tender: incapable of surviving the climatic conditions of a given region and requiring protection from frost or cold

Tuber: the thick section of a rhizome bearing nodes and buds

Variegation: foliage that has more than one color, often patched or striped or bearing leaf margins of a different color

Variety: a naturally occurring variant of a species

Index of Recommended Species Plant Names

Entries in **bold** type indicate main plant headings.

Abelia, 74
Acanthus, 30
Acer, 86
Acorus, 168
Adiantum, 152
Agastache, 27
Allium, 137
Almond, dwarf flowering. *See* Prunus
Alum root. *See* Coral bells
Amelanchier, 98
Amsonia, 32
Anemone, 42
Angel's trumpet, 147
Anise hyssop, 27
sunset, 27
wild, 27
wrinkled giant, 27
Anise tree, 53
Japanese, 53
star, 53
Apricot, Japanese flowering. *See* Prunus
Aquilegia, 35
Arachnoides, 156
Aralia, Japanese. *See* Fatsia
Arborvitae, 54
eastern, 54
oriental, 54
western, 54
Arisaema, 133
Arrowwood. *See* Viburnum
Arum, 125
Asarum, 170
Asclepias, 33

Aspidistra, 149
Aster, 28
climbing, 28
frikart, 28
great, 28
New England, 28
New York, 28
white wood, 28
Athyrium, 158
Aucuba, 79
Autumn fern, 148
Azalea. *See* **Rhododendron**

Baptisia, 29
Bear's breeches, 30
common, 30
spiny, 30
Beautyberry, 55
American, 55
Japanese, 55
Betula, 96
Bignonia, 118
Bishop's hat. *See* Epimedium
Black lily turf. *See* Mondo grass
Black-eyed Susan, 31
Blanket flower, 11
Bletilla, 127
Blue star flower, 32
downy, 32
Bluebell, Spanish. *See* Spanish squill
Blue-mist shrub, 56
Boston ivy. *See* **Virginia creeper**

Boxwood, 57
common, 57
edging, 57
Korean, 57
Brassica, 16
Busy Lizzie. *See* Impatiens
Butter daisy, 12
Butterfly weed, 33
Buxus, 57

Calamagrostis, 154
Calibrachoa, 25
Callicarpa, 55
Camellia, 58
Japanese, 58
sasanqua, 58
tea-oil, 58
Canna lily, 126
Cardinal climber. *See* Ipomoea
Carefree Beauty, 107
Carex, 164
Carolina jessamine, 115
Carolina silverbell, 59
Caryopteris, 56
Cast iron plant, 149
Catharanthus, 19
Cedar, 60
atlas, 60
blue atlas, 60
deodar, 60
of Lebanon, 60
Cedar, eastern red. *See* Juniper
Cedar, white. *See* Arborvitae

Cedrus, 60
Cephalotaxus, 91
Cercis, 94
Chaenomeles, 67
Chamaecyparis, 65
Cherry, Cornelian. *See* Dogwood
Cherry, Formosan. *See* Prunus.
Cherry, Higan. *See* Prunus
Cherry, Yoshino. *See* Prunus
Chimonanthus, 70
Chinese ground orchid, 127
Chionanthus, 71
Chives, 137
Christmas fern, 150
Chrysanthemum, 34
silver and gold, 34
Chrysogonum, 155
Cinnamon fern, 151
Clematis, 116
Climbing hydrangea, 117
Coleus, 13
Colocasia, 129
Columbine, 35
alpine, 35
European, 35
hybrid, 35
wild, 35
Common Blush China. *See* Old Blush

Common maid-
enhair fern, 152
  Northern, 152
  Southern, 152
Coneflower, 36
  purple, 36
Coneflower, cut-
  leaf. *See* Black-
  eyed Susan
Coral bells, 37
Coreopsis, 50
  lance, 50
  mouse-eared, 50
  rose, 50
  thread leaf, 50
Coreopsis. See
  Tickseed
Cornus, 64
Cosmos, 14
  sulphur, 14
Cotinus, 100
Cranberrybush,
  European. *See*
  Viburnum
Crapemyrtle, 61
  Japanese, 61
Creeper, Japanese.
  See Virginia
  creeper
Cross vine, 118
Cryptomeria, 62
Cucumber tree.
  See Magnolia
Cyclamen, 131

Daffodil, 128
Daisy, Michael-
  mas. *See* Aster
Daisy, Shasta. *See*
  Chrysanthe-
  mum
Danae, 92
*Datura & Brug-
  mansia,* 147
Dawn redwood,
  63

Daylily, 38
Deutzia, 99
Dianthus, 47
Dionaea, 169
Dogwood, 64
  Chinese, 64
  flowering, 64
  Kousa, 64
Dryopteris, 148

Echinacea, 36
Elephant's ear, 129
Epimedium, 153
Evergreen wiste-
  ria, 119

Fairy, The, 114
False cypress, 65
  Hinoki, 65
  Japanese, 65
  Sawara, 65
  threadleaf, 65
Fan flower, 15
Fatsia, 66
  Japanese, 66
Feather reed
  grass, 154
  Foerster's, 154
Fée des neiges *See*
  Iceberg
Fennel, 138
Fern, flowering.
  See Cinnamon
  fern
Fern, royal. *See*
  Cinnnamon
  fern
Flowering cab-
  bage, 16
Flowering quince,
  67
  common, 67
Foeniculum, 138
Forsythia, 68
Fothergilla, 69
  dwarf, 69

large, 69
Fragrant winter-
  sweet, 70
Fringe tree, 71
  Chinese, 71
  white, 71

Gaillardia, 11
Gardenia, 72
Gaura, 39
  white, 39
Gelsemium, 115
Geranium, straw-
  berry. *See*
  Strawberry
  begonia
Ginger, arrow-leaf.
  See Wild ginger
Ginger, Shuttle-
  worth. *See* Wild
  ginger
Ginkgo, 73
Glossy abelia, 74
Goldenrain tree, 75
Grancy graybeard.
  See Fringe tree
Grape hyacinth,
  130
  Armenian, 130
  common, 130
Grass, mist. *See*
  Muhly grass
Grass, monkey. *See*
  Mondo grass
Green and gold,
  155

Hakonechloa,
  157
Halesia, 59
Hamamelis, 106
Hardy cyclamen,
  131
Hellebore, 40
  bear's foot, 40
Helleborus, 40

Hemerocallis, 38
Heuchera, 37
Hibiscis, 97
Holly fern, 156
Holly, 76
  American, 76
  Chinese, 76
  Japanese, 76
  winterberry, 76
  Yaupon, 76
Holly, false. *See*
  Osmanthus
Holly, Oregon
  grape. *See*
  Mahonia
Honeysuckle, yel-
  low. *See* Trum-
  pet honeysuckle
Hosta, 41
Hyacinth, wood.
  See Spanish
  squill
Hyacinthoides,
  136
Hydrangea, 77
  bigleaf, 77
  garden, 77
  oakleaf, 77
  P.G., 77
  panicle, 77
  smooth, 77

Iceberg, 108
Ilex, 76
Illicium, 53
Impatiens, 17
  New Guinea, 17
Indian hawthorn,
  78
Indigo, false blue.
  See Baptisia
Indigo, white wild.
  See Baptisia
Ipomoea, 120
Iris, 132
  copper, 132

dwarf crested, 132
Japanese rooftop, 132
Siberian, 132
Virginia, 132
yellow flag, 132

Jack-in-the-pulpit, 133
Japanese anemone, 42
Japanese aucuba, 79
dwarf, 79
Japanese cleyera, 80
Japanese forest grass, 157
Japanese kerria, 81
Japanese painted fern, 158
Juncus, 159
Juneberry. See Serviceberry
Juniper, 82
Chinese, 82
creeping, 82
Japanese garden, 82
Rocky Mountain, 82
singleseed, 82
Juniperus, 82

Kalmia, 87
Kerria, 81
Kniphofia, 48
Knockout, 109
Koelreuteria, 75

Lablab, 122
Lady Banks Rose, 110
Lagerstroemia, 61

Lantana, 18
Laurel, Alexandrian. See Poet's laurel
Laurel, Carolina cherry. See Prunus
Laurel, English cherry. See Prunus
Lenten rose. See Hellebore
Licorice plant. See Anise hyssop
Lilium, 134
Lily of the valley shrub. See Pieris
Lily, 134
Formosa, 134
Lily, hurricane. See Magic lily
Lily, spider. See Magic lily
Lonicera, 123
Loropetalum, 83
Lungwort, 43
long-leaved, 43
Lycoris, 135

Madagascar periwinkle, 19
Magic lily, 135
Magnolia, 84
ashe, 84
bigleaf, 84
saucer, 84
Southern, 84
star, 84
Mahonia, 85
creeping, 85
leatherleaf, 85
Maple, 86
amur, 86
full-moon, 86
hedge, 86
Japanese, 86

paper-bark, 86
red, 86
Marjoram. See Oregano
Maypops. See Passion vine
Melampodium, 12
Mentha, 139
Metasequoia, 63
Mexican sunflower, 20
Millettia, 119
Mint, 139
chocolate, 139
orange, 139
peppermint, 139
spearmint, 139
Mondo grass, 160
Monthly Rose. See Old Blush
Moonflower. See Ipomoea
Morning glory. See Ipomoea
Mosquito plant. See Anise hyssop
Moss rose, 21
Mother of thousands. See Strawberry begonia
Mountain laurel, 87
sheep, 87
Muhlenbergia, 161
Muhly grass, 161
Muhly, hairy awn. See Muhly grass
Muhlygrass, gulf. See Muhly grass
Muhlygrass, pink. See Muhly grass
Muhlygrass, purple. See Muhly grass

Muscari, 130

Narcissus, 128
New Dawn, 111

Oak, 88
live, 88
pin, 88
scarlet, 88
white, 88
Ocimum, 145
Old Blush, 112
Olive, fragrant tea. See Osmanthus
Ophiopogon, 160
Oregano, 140
Greek, 140
Origanum, 140
Ornamental purslane. See Moss rose
Osmanthus, 89
Fortune's, 89
holly, 89
Osmunda, 151

Pachysandra, 162
Paeonia, 44
Pansy, 22
Parsley, 141
Parson's Pink China. See Old Blush
Parthenocissus, 124
Passiflora, 121
Passion flower, 121
blue, 121
Peony, 44
Perennial salvia, 45
Persian shield, 23
Petroselinum, 141
Petunia, 24
Philadelphus, 103

Phlox, 46
  creeping, 46
  early, 46
  garden, 46
  moss, 46
  summer, 46
  woodland, 46
Pieris, 90
Pinks, 47
  allwood, 47
  cheddar, 47
  cottage, 47
  maiden, 47
Pitcher plants, 163
  hooded, 163
  parrot, 163
  yellow, 163
Plum yew, 91
  Japanese, 91
Poet's laurel, 92
Polygonatum, **166**
Polystichum, **150**
Portulaca, **21**
Prunus, 93
Pulmonaria, **43**
**Purple hyacinth
  bean, 122**

**Queen Elizabeth,
  113**
Quercus, **88**

Red hot poker, 48
Redbud, 94
  Chinese, 94
  eastern, 94
Rhaphiolepis, **78**
Rhododendron, 95
River birch, 96
  European white,
  96
Rosemary, 142
Rose-of-sharon, 97
Rosmarinus, **142**
Rudbeckia, **31**
Rumex, **144**

Rush, hard. *See*
  Juncus
Rush, Japanese.
  See Sweet flag
Rush. *See* Juncus

Sage, 143
Sage, azure. *See*
  Perennial salvia
Sage, Bethlehem.
  See Lungwort
Salvia, **45, 143**
Sarracenia, **163**
Saxifraga, **167**
Scaevola, **15**
Sedge, 164
  Gray's, 164
  leatherleaf, 164
  New Zealand
  hair, 164
  seersucker, 164
  striped broad-
  leaved, 164
Sedum, 165
  autumn joy, 165
  purple autumn,
  165
Serviceberry, 98
  apple, 98
  downy, 98
  shadblow, 98
**Slender deutzia,
  99**
Smoketree, 100
Snowbell, 101
  American, 101
  Japanese, 101
**Solomon's seal,
  166**
  fragrant, 166
  silver stripe, 166
  small, 166
Sorrel, 144
  common, 144
  French, 144
Spanish squill, 136

Spiderwort, 49
Spirea, 102
  bridal wreath,
  102
  Vanhoutte, 102
Spurge, Allegheny.
  See Pachysandra
Spurge, Japanese.
  See Pachysandra
Stonecrop, purple
  autumn. *See*
  Sedum
Stonecrop, two-
  row. *See* Sedum
**Strawberry bego-
  nia, 167**
Strobilanthes, **23**
Styrax, **101**
Sweet basil, 145
  holy, 145
  sacred, 145
Sweet flag, 168
  dwarf, 168
**Sweet mock
  orange, 103**
  virginal, 103
Sweet potato vine.
  See Ipomoea
Symphyotrichum,
  28

Tea plant. *See*
  Camellia
Ternstroemia, **80**
Texas humming-
  bird mint. *See*
  Anise hyssop
Thrift. *See* Phlox
Thuja, **54**
Thyme, 146
  common, 146
  lemon-scented,
  146
Thymus, **146**
Tickseed, 50
Tithonia, **20**

Toad lily, 51
  Japanese, 51
Tradescantia, **49**
**Trailing petunia,
  25**
Tricyrtis, **51**
**Trumpet honey-
  suckle, 123**

Venus flytrap, 169
Verbena, 52
  garden, 52
  rose, 52
Viburnum, 104
  doublefile, 104
  Korean spice,
  104
Vine, Cypress. *See*
  Ipomoea
Viola, **22**
**Virginia creeper,
  124**

Weigela, 105
Wild ginger, 170
  Canada, 170
  European, 170
Wild sweet
  William. *See*
  Phlox
Winterberry. *See*
  Holly
Wisteria, summer.
  See Evergreen
  wisteria
Witch hazel, 106
  Chinese, 106
  common, 106
Woodbine. *See*
  Virginia creeper

Zinnia, 26
  Mexican, 26
  narrow-leaf, 26
  spreading, 26

Author Biographies

Pam Beck is a freelance garden writer, photographer and popular lecturer. She has regularly published articles in *Carolina Gardener Magazine* since 1993 and is also currently writing for *Wakefield* and *Wake Living Magazines*. Pam teaches residential landscaping for Wake Technical Community College's Adult Continuing Education Program; she is a local garden scout for *Better Homes & Gardens Magazine*; and she currently serves on the board of advisors of the J C Raulston Arboretum, in Raleigh, North Carolina. A member of the Garden Writers Association of America, she wrote "Perennially Yours," a gardening column for Raleigh's *News & Observer*, for five years and was honored by the *News & Observer* as "Tarheel of the Week" in May 1997. Her free time is spent gardening at her home on Falls Lake in Wake Forest, NC, with her husband, Mike, and assorted furry, four-legged assistants.

Laura Peters is a certified Master Gardener with 17 gardening books to her credit. She has gained valuable experience in every aspect of the horticultural industry in a career that has spanned more than 18 years. She enjoys sharing her practical knowledge of organic gardening, plant varieties and gardening products with fellow gardeners.

Acknowledgments

I would like to first thank Tony and Michelle Avent and their Plant Delights Nursery for enabling my plant acquisition habit and for suggesting this collaboration. Thank you to all of my garden teachers and mentors who are too many to name individually, but some of whom are: Betty Perry, Erv Evans, the North Carolina Master Gardener Program and N C Cooperative Extension, the faculty and staff of the Department of Horticultural Science at North Carolina State University, Wake Technical Community College, the J C Raulston Arboretum, Duke Gardens, the University of North Carolina at Chapel Hill Botanical Garden, my friends at *Carolina Gardener Magazine* and *Better Homes & Gardens Magazine*, the numerous "soil sisters" who have swapped plants and knowledge with me since before we all had gray hair, the Garden Writers Association, my hard-working co-author Laura Peters and the wonderful folks at Lone Pine Publishing, the garden centers who hired and trained me, my students who always teach me, my in-laws and out-laws, but especially my husband, Mike, and children, Celeste and Taylor, who always believed and encouraged my passion for all things green and growing. —*Pam Beck*

A big thanks to my parents, Gary and Lucy Peters and my friends for their endless encouragement and support all these years. I would also like to thank Pam Beck for her enthusiasm, warm heart, laughter and immense knowledge of everything North Carolina. Pam was right when she said that NC was the gardening Mecca of the south. I also learned that North Carolina isn't filled just with beautiful gardens, but also with some of the kindest people I've had the pleasure to meet. The following people and places embraced this project and did everything in their power to assist me in my travels and to answer all of my questions. Thanks to the JC Raulston Arboretum, the University of NC at Chapel Hill NC Botanical Gardens, Brock Chisholm and The Arboretum New Hanover County in Wilmington, Linda Lawson, Jim McDaniel and Airlie Gardens, Tony Avent, the Plant Delights Nursery & the Juniper Level Botanic Gardens, Raleigh Little Theater Rose Garden, Garden Supply Company and the Gardens for the Cure garden tour, Stefany and Jay Rhodes and the Front Street Inn and last but not least, Darlene and Kevin Smith. Thanks to those who allowed me to photograph their gardens, pick their brains and offered me a place to rest my weary bones. —*Laura Peters*